Date Due

The Book of Trades
[STÄNDEBUCH]

Jost Amman & Hans Sachs

17046707

with a new
Introduction by BENJAMIN A. RIFKIN

DOVER PUBLICATIONS, INC.
NEW YORK

Published in Canada by General Publishing Company, Ltd.,
30 Lesmill Road, Don Mills, Toronto, Ontario.
Published in the United Kingdom by Constable and Company, Ltd.,
10 Orange Street, London WC 2.

This Dover edition, first published in 1973, is an unabridged republication
of the German-language work (*Eygentliche Beschreibung Aller Stände
auff Erden*, etc.) originally published by Sigmund Feyerabend in Frankfurt
am Main in 1568. The following English-language material has been
specially prepared for the present edition: a Preface and Introduction (with
26 additional illustrations) by Benjamin A. Rifkin; a Note on the Text and
the Translations; prose summaries of the 114 poems by Hans Sachs; a verse
translation of the "Conclusion"; and an Index of Ranks and Occupations.
The publisher is grateful to Mr. Albert E. Lownes for making his copy of
the original edition available for reproduction.

International Standard Book Number: 0-486-22886-X
Library of Congress Catalog Card Number: 72-75581

Manufactured in the United States of America
Dover Publications, Inc.
180 Varick Street
New York, N.Y. 10014

Preface

The charm and originality of the *Ständebuch* are as undeniable as largely undefinable. Yet in this essay I have attempted some approach to the origins and conceptualization of the total book as an intellectual exercise, and its role in the formularization of objective genre pictures in European art. The obvious value of the book to historians of technology could only be partially treated in this broader, and hence less specialized, survey; and, similarly, social and economic history, which both gains evidence from the *Ständebuch* and explains part of its character, is treated only slightly. Both areas can be accepted as tacit prerequisites by the careful reader, and are documented in the footnotes. This same reader will readily discover further analogues for all of my comparative illustrations. If they accord with my general categories, *laude mea!*, and if they modify them somewhat, *mea culpa!* I know a few more myself, but the hunt is half the fun, and this is not intended as a conclusive text on the *Ständebuch*.

For help received I am grateful to Veronika Birke of the Albertina, as well as the curator and staff of that august museum; to Richard E. Stone of New York University for friendly discussion about the technology shown in the *Ständebuch*; and with the deepest love, to Josephine M. G. Jonas for her unstinting patience with a crank. The only further consolation offered by a preface is here shamelessly adopted: to pay heartfelt regards to the memory of two dear friends, one my first teacher in Art History, the other a lifetime companion of my parents.

In memoriam:

Paul Zucker   Helen Eisner

B. A. R.

Contents

Introduction
to the Dover Edition

I: NUREMBERG

Originally published in 1568, Hans Sachs' and Jost Amman's *Eygentliche Beschreibung Aller Stände auff Erden* (Exact Description of All Ranks on Earth; popularly known as the *Ständebuch*) illustrates an extensive number of contemporary professions, trades and crafts. It is a valuable document for the social history of sixteenth-century Nuremberg and of the effects of urban literacy and economics on the development of art. That a popular book on trade and the crafts was first created in Nuremberg was almost inevitable. The city held commercial primacy in Germany, indeed in all Europe, as an old proverb celebrated: *Nürnbergs Tand/ Geht durch alle Land* ("Nuremberg's hand [literally: trinkets]/ Through every land"). The real wealth of the city depended upon her adventurous merchants and highly skilled craftsmen whose guilds watchfully guarded the strict quality of their work. Willingly branded as cowards, these burghers and their council preferred the bribe and compromise in politics to outbreaks of war that disrupted trade.

Thus the city prospered until late in the sixteenth century, unparalleled in its splendor: *Nihil magnificentius, nihil ornatius tota Europa reperias* (Nothing more magnificent or splendid is to be found anywhere in Europe), wrote the Italian visitor Aeneas Sylvius (Pope Pius II from 1458 to 1464). He was deeply impressed by the contrast between this city of merchants and manufacture and the comparative squalor of the more provincial outposts of feudalism: "When one comes from Lower Franconia and perceives this glorious city, its splendor seems truly magnificent. When one enters it, one's original impression is confirmed by the beauty of the streets and the fitness of the houses ... the burghers' dwellings seem to have been built for princes. In truth, the kings of Scotland would gladly be housed so luxuriously as the ordinary citizen of Nuremberg." Mercantile prosperity held other attractions for some. The mathematician Johannes

Müller, called Regiomontanus, settled in the city in 1471, the year of Albrecht Dürer's birth, for, he explained: "it was there that I could find without difficulty all the peculiar instruments necessary for astronomy, and it is there easiest for me to keep in touch with all the learned of all countries, for Nuremberg, thanks to the perpetual journeyings of her merchants, may be counted the center of Europe."[1]

Typically enough, the author of the *Ständebuch,* Hans Sachs, was not a poet by profession but a shoemaker; this he declared in a rough hewn but buoyant couplet: *Hans Sachs war ein Schuh-/Macher und Poet dazu* (Hans Sachs was a shoe-/ Maker and a poet too). Celebrated by Wagner as one of the *Meistersinger von Nürnberg,* Sachs wrote verses—some 6205 pieces in all!—that are generally goodnatured (save for some polemics against the Pope), slightly sarcastic about obvious evils, and mildly preachy in tone. Like his counterpart in seventeenth-century Holland, Jacob Cats, Sachs chiefly aimed to provide painless moral instruction. It is thus as a didactic work that the *Ständebuch* must first be considered, although its picture cycle also developed a basic branch of genre art.

II: TEXT AND ILLUSTRATION

The combination of didactic text and explanatory illustrations was an ancient one that survived in the medieval scriptorium. Certain disciplines, such as mathematics and astronomy, herbology and medicine, were always better taught with a diagram or picture than by discourse alone. Nor was this altered by the invention of the press, for the earliest printed illustrated books simply used woodcuts in place of, and at first in direct imitation of, the painted miniature. By cutting away those portions of a design not intended for printing, the block cutter produced a raised replica of the artist's drawing which, when fitted into the press and inked along with the metal letters, printed clear and economical illustrations. Thus many Renaissance books carried the last charges of medieval scholasticism. A paradigmatic instance is the mid-thirteenth-century compendium of learning drawn from ancient authorities by the Englishman Bartholomaeus Anglicus: *De Proprietatibus Rerum.*[2] This was then translated into English in the late fourteenth century by John of Trevisa, and published at the end of the fifteenth century by Wynkyn de Worde as *All the Propytees of Thynges* (Westminster, 1495). The woodcuts in this edition were borrowed from the earlier French translation printed in Lyons in 1482, the same year that a Flemish scribe and miniaturist produced the handsome manuscript version now in the British Museum (Royal Mss. 15 E. ii, iii); a Dutch translation of 1485 (Haarlem) also used the Lyons blocks, while an unillustrated Latin text was printed in Germany in 1488. Thus in a matter of less than two decades one manuscript and four printed versions, in four languages, appeared, most with illustrations.

This rapid expansion of the production and consumption of books in the last decades of the fifteenth century was not always considered synonymous with an increase of learning. The publisher and satirist Sebastian Brant censured the vain assemblage of libraries first in his *Narrenschiff* (Ship of Fools; Strassburg, 1494), where a bibliophile admits: "Of splendid books I own no end,/ But few which I can comprehend." This repeats an old trope of moral indignation against erudite pretense. It can be found voiced by a Parisian preacher of the thirteenth century in a sermon against the thriving market in elaborately bound books which students urged their parents to buy but apparently read with less ardor. "What knowledge is this," the preacher asked, "which thieves may steal, mice or moths eat up, fire or water destroy?"[3] Yet Brant was not addressing the small community of thirteenth-century students, but the middle class of several countries.[4] His complaint signals a broadly expanded audience for printed books, albeit one in need of chiding for its indulgence in unread libraries. This audience expanded once more in the next generation, which felt the full effects of the movements for a vernacular Gospel and liturgy, expressed in part by the *Devotio moderna* of the Brethren of the Common Life and given irresistible impetus by Martin Luther and the Reformation.

It has been wisely noted that more was quite probably written and read during these few years than ever before: Luther's works are in seventy-one volumes, Melanchthon's in twenty-eight, and Erasmus' in nine immense folios of about a thousand pages each. These were only the crest of a veritable flood of pamphlets, broadsides and similar ephemera, often illustrated.[5] This literature provoked an urgent literacy among the middle and artisan classes, who now encouraged schooling through guild support. Both the Kingdom of Heaven and a better social situation were opened to these people by education, so that a new pedagogy began to develop alongside the curriculum of humanism.[6]

In response to Luther's letter to the German cities asking them to found schools, Nuremberg in 1525 invited Philip Melanchthon's assistance in creating a gymnasium. After a brilliant beginning, this school floundered, leaving the education of the middle-class laity to its usual chances in the home. There were a few rough grammars available in the vernacular, but no program of readings comparable to that established by the humanists for the gymnasium student of Latin. Thus many illustrated books not specifically intended for primary instruction began to serve as instructional readers (although the first true illustrated primer, Joannes Commenius' *Orbis Sensualium Pictus,* did not appear until 1658). These works are typified by Gregorius Reisch's *Margarita philosophica* ("Pearls of Wisdom"), which appeared in numerous editions after 1503.[7] Containing moral precepts, explanations of the arts and some science, it provided an illustrated and abridged review of medieval learning for beginning scholars.

By the middle of the sixteenth century the older school texts were largely outmoded by a rapid expansion of knowledge in the sciences. In the course of about a year, the entire structures of antique botany, anatomy and astronomy were altered: Leonhard Fuchs' *De Historia Stirpium Commentarii* (Basel, 1542) replaced Dioscorides as the basic authority on plant life; Andreas Vesalius' *De Humani Corporis Fabrica* (Basel, 1543) established a new methodology for anatomical research, long dominated by Galen; Nicolaus Copernicus' *De Revolutionibus Orbium Coelestium* (Nuremberg, 1543) first proposed the heliocentric planetary system in contradiction to Ptolemy. Certainly the first two depended largely upon carefully prepared illustrations for their effective revision of established learning, and even Copernicus' theory was demonstrated by diagrams.

The study of geography and ethnography was similarly enhanced by the printed picture, while an increase in the literate public made large atlas publications possible. Since the Middle Ages curiosity about the farther corners of the earth had been satisfied with travelers' accounts, indiscriminately read whether accurate or fantastic. The artist-reporter, long the private emissary of the courts, now could serve the public as an observer on exotic journeys, preparing his drawings for publication as prints. Thus Breytenbach's rather pedantic account of Jerusalem and its sites, the *Sanctae Peregrinationes* (Mainz, 1486), is largely remembered for its illustrations by Erhard Reuwich; a more consistently reliable set of drawings was made in Turkey in 1533 by Pieter Coeck van Aelst, although they were only published twenty years later as the *Moeurs et Fachons des Turcs.*[8] Modern geography actually began with the publication of Abraham Ortelius' *Theatrum Orbis Terra-*

rum in Antwerp, 1570; this replaced fantastic narratives and schematized maps with accurate data and precise cartography. Ortelius' engraver, Francis Hogenberg, was with others simultaneously preparing the plates for Georg Braun's immense *Civitates Orbis Terrarum* (Cologne, I–V: 1572–82; VI: 1618). This included with its many maps entire city vistas, and illustrations of local customs and costumes. These geographies and related books on costume, history and biography were loosely classified as cosmography by contemporary writers.

The cosmography served as a supplemental reader and textbook both for the student and interested adult. In his treatise on education, *The Book Named the Governor* (1531), Thomas Elyot prescribed just such fare for the emergent personality of the Renaissance child, while also evoking a charming image of the adult reader:

> Albeit there is none so good learning as the demonstration of cosmography of material figures and instruments, having a good instructor. And surely this lesson is both pleasant and necessary. For what pleasure is it in one hour to behold those realms, cities, seas, rivers, and mountains, that scarcely in an old man's life cannot be journeyed and pursued; what incredible delight is taken in beholding the diversities of people, beasts, fowls, fishes, trees, fruits, and herbs: to know the sundry manners and conditions of people, and the variety of their natures, and that in a warm study or parlour, without peril of the sea or danger of long and painful journeys: I cannot tell what more pleasure should happen to a gentle wit, than to behold in his own house everything that within all the world is contained.[9]

Thus the primary role of the *Ständebuch*, with its descriptions of the "sundry manners and conditions of people," is explained by the general interest shown in the nature of people's lives, quite unprecedented in the antique literature and medieval scholastic texts preferred by the more academic humanists. Indeed, a more primitive book describing ranks and trades had already appeared which was specifically intended for the young scholar: *Ain nützlich Büchlein ... Da eiñ all Stand der menschen begriffen/ ordenlich uñ mit fleyss/ ... den Jungen fruchtbarlich zůlessen* (A Useful Little Book ... Containing All the Ranks of Humanity/ Properly and Diligently/ ... Profitable Reading for the Young), published in Augsburg, 1531.

It is also not amiss to notice that the *Ständebuch* appeared in the same year as the considerably expanded second edition of Vasari's *Vite*, which also signals the new status given the artist and artisan in intellectual circles.[10] Yet although a member of the cosmography genus in many ways, the *Ständebuch* is more specifically a hybrid derived from the ancient encyclopedia and later medieval treatises on craft technology. Its organization, sources and moral purpose are evolved from these older traditions, which must be isolated in examining its very real innovation as a work of social portraiture and craft genre.

III: MEDIEVAL ENCYCLOPEDIAS AND THE MECHANICAL ARTS

The encyclopedic omnium gatherum was devised by the Roman scholars who sought to absorb and later to preserve Hellenistic learning; in this form knowledge was largely codified for preservation by medieval scholastics until the Renaissance. Their encyclopedias usually treated chronology, astronomy and natural science, something of history, law and the liberal arts; they rarely contained specifics of the agrarian or domestic crafts, or technological instruction—which was reserved for specialized treatises. In his preface to the *Ständebuch*, after a needlessly verbose definition of God, the publisher Sigmund Feyerabend praised the *Historia Naturalis* of Pliny the Elder (23/24–79 A.D.) as a perfect model of antique learning; Feyerabend had just published in 1565 a German translation of Books VII to XI of Pliny's work, which was the only important ancient encyclopedia to survive the Middle Ages almost intact. These five sections dealt with anthropology and physiology (VII), and with zoology; they were illustrated by Jost Amman. Yet Feyèrabend felt that there still remained an immense variety of human arts and crafts, not covered by Pliny, which also served God. To expound the virtue of these the *Ständebuch* was begun, probably in the same year as the publication of the Pliny, for the date 1565 can be read on the side of the press in Amman's woodcut of the printer's workshop, Plate 19. Although an appendage to Pliny, the *Ständebuch* satisfies, perhaps inadvertently, the requisites for knowledge of people proposed by Pliny's predecessor Varro (114–27 B.C.) in the considerable portions of his *Rerum Humanarum et Divinarum Antiquitates* (now known only in a few fragmentary quotations) concerned with human actions. Of each subject Varro would ask four basic questions: who performs, what is the action, where and when? In an informal way, the *Ständebuch* answered just these questions.[11]

The mechanical arts, which would include the crafts that occupy most of the *Ständebuch,* were not mentioned in the classical encyclopedias or their earliest medieval imitations. They seem to have first appeared in Hugo of St. Victor's *Didascalicon de Studio Legendi,* a rather clearly presented guide for students that recommends readings and defines the branches of learning; composed in c. 1130, and largely based upon the older encyclopedias of Isidore and his followers, the *Didascalicon* achieved a greater precision in dealing with mathematics and science than had its immediate predecessors. To the traditional liberal arts Hugo added seven corresponding mechanical arts, which were: *lanificium,* textile and leather work; *armatura,* weaponry and manufacture in wood, stone and metal; *navigatio,* shipping and trade; *agricultura,* agronomy and husbandry; *venatio,* game hunting, fishing and food preparation; *medicina;* and *theatrica,* the arts of entertainment. Citing Aristotle and Boethius as his sources, Hugo gave an explanation of each craft's origins as the imitation of a natural process to satisfy a human need: thus we clothe ourselves by imitating the tree's growth of bark. Hugo's work was soon imitated: Dominicus Gundissalinus, Michael Scot and Robert Kilwardby each accepted the new order of mechanical arts, identifying them with their most similar liberal art.[12]

The seven mechanical arts again appeared in the mid-thirteenth-century *Speculum Doctrinale* (Mirror of Instruction), the first part of Vincent of Beauvais' compendious and extremely influential *Speculum Maius* (Great, or Universal, Mirror). In part, the acceptance of this series into the traditional contents of the encyclopedia reflects an intellectual response to the growing power of trade and manufacture in the cities. At Chartres, as an instance approximately contemporary to the *Speculum,* the cathedral's fabric was largely financed by nineteen guilds including the drapers, bakers and tanners. Each was suitably commemorated in a stained-glass window showing an artisan at work or holding the tool symbolic of his trade and coupled as donor to a Biblical subject.[13]

The theological explanation for the inclusion of the mechanical arts in an encyclopedia was simple: as man's soul suffered darkness after his fall, so too his body was subjected to the harshness of life outside of Paradise; as the Seven Liberal Arts and Seven Virtues lead the mind and soul back to grace, so too the varieties of work relieve the body of its subjugation to necessity. Thus Vincent framed seven *necessitates:* seven mechanical arts which are companions to the liberal arts and virtues, and include textile crafts, architecture (instead of Hugo's *armatura*), navigation, agriculture, hunting, medicine and *theatrica*. An early programmatic representation of the concept of redemption through work appeared in the reliefs on the lower story of the campanile at Santa Maria del Fiore, the Cathedral of Florence. Designed, perhaps with Giotto's partial assistance, and largely executed by Andrea Pisano between 1334 and 1343, the hexagonal panels include a Hercules, as the symbol of virtuous labor, and Adam and Eve, with whom obligatory labor originated: the burden of these labors is continued in the generation of Noah, who is seen as the representation of viniculture, Jubal the musician and Tubalcain the blacksmith. The whole cycle closely approximates the encyclopedic order of Hugo or Vincent, and includes figures of agriculture, navigation and medicine; a shepherd and a carter; a sculptor and a painter and a geographer; an astronomer and a scene of Daedalus' flight. Various technical subjects, such as methods of agriculture, weaving and smithery, engineering, painting and glazing, had already appeared in Italy a generation earlier as *exempla* in the sermons of the Dominican friar Giovanni da San Gimignano (d. 1323); these he transcribed in an encyclopedia for other preachers.[14]

The mechanical arts were again moralized in the later fifteenth-century *Speculum Vitae Humanae* (Mirror of Human Life), a didactic and encyclopedic treatise by the Bishop Roderigo of Zamora. Substantially a reworking of older texts, this work was first printed in a German translation by Günther Zainer of Augsburg in *c.* 1475/6 as the *Spiegel des menschlichen Lebens.* Its woodcuts, by an Ulm artist, were used again in a subsequent German edition of 1479, the French edition printed in Lyons, 1482, and the Spanish version printed in Saragossa, 1492.[15] The seven mechanical arts, six of which had an accompanying illustration, followed the traditional ordering of the encyclopedias: textile and leather work; metal, stone and wood carving and crafts; trade and business; farming; hunting and cuisine; medicine and barbering; and the arts of entertainment.

Thus a formularized series of representations for the categories of work evolved over a period of three centuries. Yet more subtle distinctions in the stratification of society were also occurring, although with little immediate or direct influence on art, which remained subservient to the latent dreams of chivalry nurtured in the courts. The mutant states of men aroused great anger in the early thirteenth century, when an English preacher railed: "God made the clergy, knights and la-

Fig. 1. Andrea Pisano, *Tubalcain*. Relief sculpture, c. 1334–1343, Florence, Santa Maria del Fiore, campanile. (Courtesy Alinari—Art Reference Bureau)

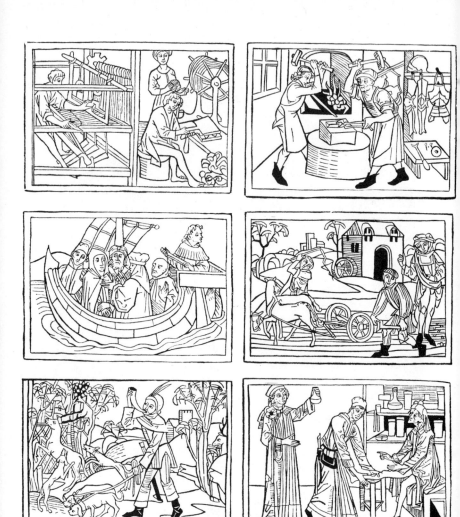

Figs. 2–7. Ulm Master, *Six Mechanical Arts: Textile Work, Smithing, Navigation, Agriculture, Hunting and Medicine.* Woodcut illustrations, c. 1475, from Rodericus Zamorensis, *Speculum Vitae Humanae.*

borers, but the devil made the burghers and usurers." A similar sentiment can be found in the contemporary German poet Freidank's *Von
Wuocher* (Of Usury), reflecting a general intellectual distrust of the
counter-feudal society.[16] By the beginning of the new century a new
attitude informed the pulpit and popular moralist, who adapted the
explication of craft work offered by the encyclopedias to a new urban
morality.

In Germany, this current was typified by the early fourteenth-
century poem *Der Renner* (The Runner, or Universal Traveler), the
work of a retired schoolteacher, Hugo von Trimberg. In this lengthy
description of and prescription for the moral state of mankind, von
Trimberg found all the crafts and most trades equally honorable, as
they served in alleviating the bitter plight of fallen man. He suggests
that there are two paths of education, one in the liberal arts and the
other in the crafts, which both provide for human needs:

> Art, however, has two paths;
> One raises the soul toward God,
> The other prepares the needs of the body.
> Learned people stand on the first,
> Handworkers travel the second.
> The first expiates ignorance,
> The second expiates sorrow.

Furthermore, although the *hantwercliute* (handworkers) do not know
the liberal arts, their labor and skill sustain their fellowmen and thus
profit their souls.[17]

The normative values expressed by von Trimberg and many other
medieval homilists were retained by later German writers as a valid
paradigm of social criticism. The special form of satire evolved by the
generation of Brant and Murner on the eve of the Reformation was
concurrent to a revival of this older literature: Brant himself published
in 1509 an expanded and illustrated redaction of Freidank's *Beschei-
denheit,* while a similarly revised edition of von Trimberg's *Der Renner*
appeared in 1549, nineteen years before the *Ständebuch.* The essential
complaints of the early homilists had not altered to any great degree
in the intervening centuries, although contempt and irony came to
replace anger and indignation as the mode of expression in the popular publications which replaced the pulpit. The moral lode of the
Ständebuch is not far from this literature, although it echoes it in more
genial phrases.

IV: MORAL PURPOSE IN THE *STÄNDEBUCH*

As a poet, Sachs was as dependent as the satirists upon medieval traditions: his loving poem in praise of his second wife Barbara Harscherin, *Der Künstliche Frauenlob* (The Artful Praise of Women), is a direct imitation of the phrases and metre of the lyric thirteenth-century *Minnesang*. Sachs' major form, the *Meistergesang* (Master Song), was a ritualized and rather rhetorical autumnal quiescence of the *Minnesang*; Sachs wrote the formal code for this verse style, although he was never rigid in applying it to his own work. A devoted follower of Martin Luther, whom he styled the "Nightingale of Wittenberg," Sachs translated large portions of both Testaments into German. In most of his writings, save for a few virulent attacks upon the Pope, he coupled mild wit with gentle reproach in an effort at edifying instruction. And the *Ständebuch* too is graced with a moral purpose, drawn from an old tradition, and aimed at the newly literate artisan class.

This intention of the *Ständebuch* is stated in Sachs' concluding verse: it is a model for the great varieties of trade and craft people which ought to be profitably observed; they should refrain from idleness, give true work and measure, and avoid all vices; praise and love the God Who feeds us all; and know that whoever runs an evil business, no matter what the temporal rewards, loses all in the end. These were reasonable precepts for a productive middle class which thrived on mutual responsibility; they do not differ from similar admonitions which Albrecht Dürer wrote in his letters to Pirckheimer (although the patrician Pirckheimer's morals certainly did differ from these!).[18]

As a model of behavior and source of *exempla* for the artisan the *Ständebuch* lacked the pessimism of the satirists; its moral is implied rather than larded into each passage. In condemning a very few types, such as Jews and lawyers, Sachs was following literary conventions long established in the pulpit and not describing specifically local problems. The Jew appears merely as an allegorical instance of usury, for the Jews had been dismissed from Nuremberg in 1499. Sachs' old foe the Pope is not singled out for ridicule, which is reserved only for the mendicant pilgrims among the religious orders. Here too, an older attitude is preserved, although in far less abusive language than that used by Luther in his preface to an edition of the *Liber Vagatorum* which condemned all beggars as the Devil's own.[19] The number of fools shown in the *Ständebuch* is slight in comparison to the population of Brant's

Ship of Fools, nor do they receive any particular attack. The complaints of the farmer, Plate 42, are sad echoes of the miseries already described in two thirteenth-century epics: *Meier Helmbrecht* and *Der Arme Heinrich.*[20] Finally, Sachs' anger at the lawyer who defends the malefactor is again a commonplace of moral tracts: in the *Renner,* Hugo von Trimberg finds that an honest judge is a rarer sight than a white raven or a black swan![21] Yet these earlier authors also attacked the medical profession, while Sachs, living in Paracelsus' Nuremberg, saw no evil in the work of doctors. In almost every case Sachs eschewed even established opportunities to condemn, instead citing positive and descriptive examples of man's work.

To a certain extent the *Ständebuch* sustained the hierarchal arrangement of the classes found in the encyclopedias: church and statecraft are listed first, followed by the intellectual arts of astronomy and medicine; musicians and fools are listed last, either as types of *theatricales* or as misfits in the social order. However, the major substance of the book is given to the arts and crafts of manufacture and commerce, a change in the proportioning of the mechanical arts consonant with the new urban audience. Feudal trades are almost totally absent while single woodcuts of a farmer and vintager represent agriculture. Strangely enough, the teacher is missing from the *Ständebuch.*

Thus the *Ständebuch* culminates the medieval preacher's beatification of work which had begun in the thirteenth century.[22] It was a theme which had found some expression in pictures by the end of the fifteenth century. A single leaf with a miniature attributed to Jean Bourdichon (or his circle; Paris, Ecole des Beaux-Arts) of *c.* 1500 represents the four states of society in four vignettes: a wild man's family suffering the hazards of savagery; a poor man's family enduring the misery of sloth; a carpenter's family representing the craftsman whose skills distinguish the upper from the lower ranks of mankind; and a rich, but not noble, family.[23] That a carpenter symbolizes the artisan is perhaps an intentional allusion to the trade of Joseph which supported the Holy Family; in a sense not strange to medieval typological thought, Joseph's, and thus Christ's, trade has replaced the agrarian labors of Adam, as Christ's teachings replaced the old dispensation. A more elaborate, if also more opaque, allegorical beatification of labor was couched in the vocabulary of late medieval romance by Jean Bruyant; known in both manuscript and printed editions, his *Livre du Chastel de Labour* (Book of the Castle of Labor) narrated the triumph

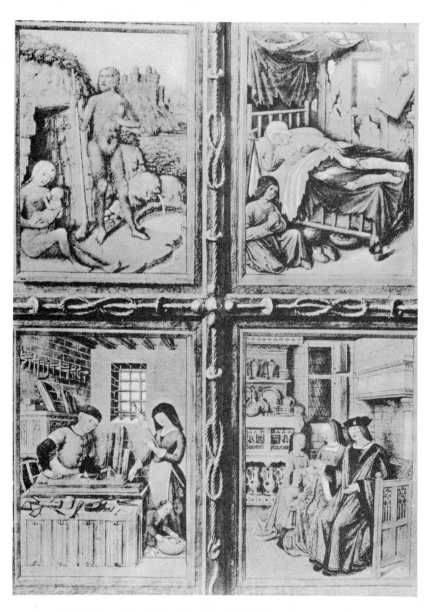

Fig. 8. Jean Bourdichon (attributed to), *The Four Stages of Human Society*. Painted miniature, c. 1500, Paris, Ecole des Beaux-Arts.

over suffering, hunger and anxiety, despite care, fraud and hatred—
inter alia!—by an artisan who learned from Wisdom and in the Castle
of Labor the virtue of industrious application.[24] In form a descendant
of the *Roman de la Rose*, and in purpose akin to *Piers Plowman* or the
Ménagier de Paris, the *Chastel* and its few illustrations of labor are an
important if dull instance of the new bourgeois use of older courtly
forms.

The order and language of the *Ständebuch* are direct and simple,
free of the convoluted imagery found in the *Chastel de Labour;* in
the *Ständebuch* it is the craftsmen themselves who replace abstract
allegories as the vehicles of moral content. Yet the virtues of bourgeois
domesticity are not ignored in this later view of artisan society: a
needle maker at his anvil is joined by his wife, partner in his trade,
who puts the needles into packets for market (Plate 76); similarly,
while a child plays before their shop a bell maker die-cuts the forms
for bells which his wife sews into form (Plate 74). Even in the few
scenes representing heavy work, most typically the casting of bells
(Plate 54), the craftsman is shown as a bench worker. Thus the *Ständebuch* illustrates and praises not work in general, but handwork of the
artisan class in particular. The importance of their social status is
easily noted in the elegant costumes which Amman assigned most of
his figures in the *Ständebuch*.

V: TECHNICAL TREATISES

The interest shown in art and science by the educated of the later
Renaissance, and the increasing need for exact instruction in increasingly complex technologies, provided an audience for a new form of
book: the handbook on a single art or science containing precise data
written in relatively unembellished prose by a professional artisan or
engineer. Thus in the generation before the *Ständebuch* the artisan
class was not only an emerging theme in art and literature, but productive of a literature special to its own pragmatic interests. Like so
much else in Renaissance science, this type of treatise had a long
medieval ancestry; special explanatory works on dyes and pigments,
preparation of glass, parchment and fabrics, and most important,
metallurgy—the arts of extraction, refining and amalgamation—were
known in surviving manuscripts since the twelfth century, the *Diverse
Arts* of Theophilus being the best known but far from the only example.
Guilds also prepared treatises on particular crafts; the now lost book

on weaving and cloth making from Ypres is a well-illustrated guide to practices and tools for fabric work; the notebook of the twelfth-century architect Villard de Honnecourt is again the best known, but also most informal, as it were, instance of a masonic album of ground-plans, tracery designs, formulae for statues and the like. Yet each of these text genres remained the private concern of the monastery, guild or lodge for which they were prepared; manuscript copies are abundant, but were never intended for public circulation.

The increasing public need for a new, vastly more complex technology altered the medieval treatise when it entered print. The early *Kunstbüchlin* (Art Booklet) was an agglomeration of mining and dyeing, metal work and painting, embellished with ornamental copy patterns for embroiderers. In the same decade, however, there appeared pattern books meant especially for the artist and tracts on amalgamation intended for the alchemist, leaving metallurgy a fairly well-defined area of expertise. Indeed, in 1540 a practicing Sienese mining engineer and metal worker, Vannuccio Biringuccio, brought out the *Pirotechnia,* an empirical series of methods for extracting, refining and casting metals; incidental to this purpose, the *Pirotechnia* also included a good deal about the sister art of pottery. In 1556 Agricola's *De Re Metallica* again revised the science of mining and metallurgy, spawning a further series of special treatises in ore-rich Bohemia. The romance of heavy instrumental machines inadvertently projected by these works fostered the fantastic devices of Jacques Besson's *Théâtre des instruments mathematiques et mechaniques,* Lyons, 1578; elaborate screw presses, lathes—one with a true mandril chuck, however—and similar devices seem more the predecessors of Piranesi's machines than contemporary inventions.[25] The *Ständebuch* has little of this machinery, but rather shares the direct interest in visual data required of the technical treatises. As these established labor as an extensively complex subject of scientific interest, Amman presented handworkers as equally significant subjects both in science and art; aside from its value then as a description of bench technology, as it were, the *Ständebuch* created the first self-sufficient cycle of craft genre pictures.

VI: JOST AMMAN AND GENRE ILLUSTRATION

Jost Amman typifies the proficiency of many Renaissance German artists in a wide range of artistic skills. The son of a professor of Latin, Greek, rhetoric and logic, he was born in Zurich, 13 June 1539. His older brother became a goldsmith, whereas Jost was trained in portrait and glass painting in the circle of Hans Asper, an imitator of Hans Holbein the Younger.[26] Although his few surviving early works closely follow local conventions, some specific contact can be recognized with the glass painter Hieronymus Lang (c. 1520–1582) in neighboring Schaffhausen. (Another Amman, the engraver Jeremias, was also active there until c. 1572.) The style of Amman's earliest drawings has occasionally been confused with Lang's; several of Amman's compositional formulae may also be derived from him. Amman's drawing (Basel, Kupferstichkabinett) for the Falkner-Irmy window of 1560 in Basel essentially repeats the composition of a window designed by Lang a decade earlier for Hans Schwartz (Cambridge, Mass., Fogg Art Museum). The woodcut in the *Ständebuch* of an ox-slaughtering, Plate 37, recalls a drawing by Lang (Stuttgart, Staatsgalerie) of the same subject for a window for Hans Houwenschilt.[27] Thus it is possible that after completing his apprenticeship in Zurich and before arriving in Basel in 1557 for a stay of three years, Amman spent some time in about 1556 in Schaffhausen. Here he might have met his contemporary Tobias Stimmer (Schaffhausen, 1539 – Strassburg, 1584), the other outstanding woodcut designer of Amman's generation in Germany and Switzerland.

By 3 March 1561 Amman had already moved from Basel and entered the studio of Virgil Solis (1514–1562), the leading woodcut artist in Nuremberg.[28] After Solis' death on 1 August 1562 Amman took responsibility for the studio, which he maintained until his own death on 17 March 1591. He married a Nuremberg widow, Barbara Wilke, in 1574, and settled in a house on the Obere Schmiedgasse; three years later he became a citizen of Nuremberg with an exemption from the regular fee. Not particularly well off despite his industry, Amman left Nuremberg only for local trips: Augsburg in 1578, Frankfurt and Heidelberg in 1583, Würzburg in 1586/7 and Altdorf in 1590. An important etcher and engraver, Amman was most prolific as a woodcut designer and draughtsman, whose drawings were executed as woodcuts by his numerous studio assistants or sold to outside artisans. His thirty years in Nuremberg were largely devoted to illustrating the immense variety of books published by the Frankfurt firm of Sigmund Feyerabend (1528–1590).[29] In the *Ständebuch* Amman's self-portrait probably appears both as a block cutter, Plate 17, and designer, Plate 16. The only contemporary account of Amman was transcribed from a former student's reminiscences by the German painter Joachim von

Fig. 9. Jost Amman, *Design for the Falkner-Irmy Window.* Drawing, 1560, Basel, Kupferstichkabinett. (Courtesy Öffentliche Kunstsammlung Basel)

Sandrart, and published in his *Teutsche Academie,* a collection of biographies of German and Netherlandish artists that was printed in 1675; after praising the good origins of Amman's family, his skill and his industriousness, Sandrart reported that: "In Frankfurt in 1616 Amman's pupil Jörg Keller recalled for me, not without reasonable wonderment, that during his four years spent in Nuremberg as a student, Amman drew so many pieces that he doubted whether all could be carted away in a hay wagon."[30]

Fig. 10. Hieronymus Lang, *Design for the Hans Schwartz Window.*
Drawing, c. 1550, Cambridge, Mass., Fogg Art Museum. (Courtesy of
the Fogg Art Museum, Harvard University, Bequest of Charles
Alexander Loeser, Esq.)

This appropriate exaggeration indicates the adaptable prolificness of Amman's art which stands in paradoxical contrast to his personal background. Raised in a humanist family, Amman's circle in Nuremberg was also among the educated. His close friend Wenzel Jamnitzer, the goldsmith and engraver to whom the *Ständebuch* was dedicated, wrote a treatise on perspective in 1568; Amman himself was presumed to have written a theoretical work on poetry, painting and architecture which has not survived.[31] Yet Amman's art was considered devoid of theoretical foundation soon after his own lifetime. In the *Teutscher Nation Herrlichkeit* (The Glory of the German Nation), published in Cologne in 1609, the cartographer, humanist and engraver Matthias Quadt von Kinckelbach divided artists into adherents of either *Leben,* i.e. traditional craft practices and direct transcription of nature, or *Geist,* i.e. the sublime rules of art that governed perspective, proportion and decorum. These categories, which haunt seventeenth-century criticism, imply a real distinction in purpose between artists mainly concerned with academic proprieties of form and ennobling subjects and sentiment, and the mundane illustrations which artists like Jost Amman prepared. Naturally enough, Amman is classed among the followers of *Leben,* as is Dürer—with reservations!—while Virgil Solis is found among the more scientifically grounded.[32]

Yet seventeenth-century academic concepts of scientific art principles failed to estimate the real purpose of Amman and his generation as illustrators. For all their enthusiasm, readers of the first printed books had tolerated a good deal of fictitious illustration in secular works; theological subjects were traditionally more clearly defined and controlled. Thus the 1809 pictures in the most elaborate illustrated incunabulum, Hartmann Schedel's *Weltchronik* (Nuremberg Chronicle), published in both a Latin and German version in 1493 by Dürer's godfather, Anton Koberger, were actually printed from 645 distinct blocks that were repeated for every appropriate instance; thus several cities share exactly the same aspect, while as many as eighteen different people have the same portrait![33] Perhaps the reader was expected to forget within a few pages an image he had seen in an earlier chapter, or more likely, he simply accepted an image without critical scepticism or comparison with its textual counterpart. The audience of the *Ständebuch* three generations later was equally curious, although somewhat less trusting. Only two of Amman's cuts are repeated, the peddler, Plate 33, as a common fool, Plate 114, and the weaver, Plate 48, as a tapestry weaver, Plate 110, and these are not illogical duplications. The relationship between Sachs' doggerel verses, compiled from iterated terms and listings of goods, and Amman's pictures, primarily of working processes, achieves a genuine balance between word and image. Without pedantic accordance with the humanist dictum *ut pictura poësis* ("as in the picture, so in the verse") propounded for emblematic illustration, there is in the *Ständebuch* a nicely complementary balance between the vocabulary of a trade given in the text and the action of a trade shown in the illustration. Then too, Amman maintains a high standard of verisimilitude in all of his pictures, generally reflecting and furthering the increasingly strict criteria for scientific illustrations emerging in his generation. As an instance, his wagonwright, Plate 89, makes a dished wheel in which the spokes are set at a bias to the hub to better distribute the stress of a load. In the frontispiece which Amman designed for the 1565 edition of Paracelsus' *Opus Chyrurgicum,* a work on surgery, medicine and anatomy published by Feyerabend, an actual public dissection with anatomy lecture is shown in progress, observed from personal attendance.[34]

Amman not only illustrated familiar texts with established picture cycles, such as works of mythology and the Bible, but an immense range of specialized subjects which had more diffuse visual precedents, if any. Aside from emblematic and costume works, Amman illustrated several books on natural history, including sections of Pliny the Elder's *Historia Naturalis* and Scheller's *Thierbuch* (Book of Animals); books on medicine, including Paracelsus' *Wund- und Arzneibuch* (Book of Wounds and Cures) and Camerarius' *Hortus Medicus,* a classic herbal. Other books included travel accounts from Turkey and Russia, studies on warfare and arms, and the *Ständebuch.* Thus, rather than turning his attention to theoretical precepts of style, Amman used his intellect to observe, gather and present visual data. Instead of subjective expression, his art aimed at the correct presentation of this information for its value in learning, applying to illustration the scientific prerequisite of making an exact description of observed phenomena.

Thus Amman's style altered more in response to changes of subject matter than changes of maturation or mood. While the large and handsome etching of a *Fireworks Display at the Castle of Nuremberg* (1570; Andr. 70) combined reportorial acumen with a topographical account, the drama of the event was instinctively matched by the print's style: a strongly animated frieze acts as a repoussoir, placing the castle and its rocket bursts in a deep spatial recess; an equally intense

Fig. 11. Jost Amman, *Fireworks Display at the Castle of Nuremberg.*
Etching, Andr. 70, 1570, Vienna, Albertina. (Courtesy Gesellschaft der
Freunde der Albertina)

chiaroscuro contrasts and isolates the centers of activity without distortion. In effect, the energized style of the etching is completely responsive to the explosive flurry of the festival itself. In the small woodcuts of the *Ständebuch* such rich exposition was unnecessary. Setting and embellishment are reduced to a minimum which presents the primary significant actions of a craftsman and details of his tools and goods with maximum clarity. The style is a schematization of Solis' small Bible prints, and Hans Holbein the Younger's Bible and *Dance of Death* series; in effect, the *Dance of Death* is also a book of human ranks. In these, and related works of the early sixteenth century, a method of woodcut design was achieved that closely conformed to the technical limitations of the block cutter. Amorphous modeling resulted from the precedence of the outline over plane; hatching patterns were evenly parallel to distinguish segments of form in a legible image rather than create atmospheric effects; features were often abbreviated to a few notations of eyebrow and nose and mouth; and a few suggestive strokes sufficed for the texture of beards, draperies and masonry. The very real efficiency of this style can be seen in the rendering of the springing turn of the glazier's body, Plate 23, which deftly spirals within the arrayed clutter of his implements and wares. Neither action nor setting takes precedence as both are formed with uniform means, achieving a stable amalgam of recognizably distinct parts.

This rather objective style was well suited to the assimilation of a variety of sources from which this single corpus was necessarily composed. Like his contemporaries, Amman both retained a vast reserve of his own drawings for continuous cannibalization into new works of art, and easily borrowed motifs from other pictures to supply particular needs. Thus Amman's pen drawing in Berlin of a seated man without any specific attributes appears as the seated farmer in the *Ständebuch,* Plate 42, knitted to another standing figure drawn from a second source, and given the explanatory tools of his trade. Similarly, Amman's mendicant pilgrim, Plate 6, is a fairly literal copy after a woodcut by the early sixteenth-century Swiss artist known as the Master DS, to which again a second figure has been added. Other less exact duplications can also be suggested as an indication of Amman's method: a pen drawing of a hunter with a dog (formerly Schickman Gallery, New York) suggests a general prototype for the cut of the hunter, Plate 44, and, with a few alterations, of the cook, Plate 39. In both, background, attributes and adjustments of posture and costume' would seem to have been added after the basic figure was determined.

Fig. 12. Jost Amman, *Seated Man*. Drawing, c. 1568, Berlin, Kupfer-stichkabinett. (Courtesy Staatliche Museen Preussischer Kulturbesitz)

Fig. 13. Master DS, *Pilgrim*. Woodcut, Bock XII, 1506.

Fig. 14. Jost Amman, *Hunter with a Dog*. Drawing, c. 1568+, formerly New York, Schickman Gallery. (Courtesy of Norman Leitman)

Yet these instances account only for the more conventional of Amman's designs in the *Ständebuch;* the largest number show instead a sophisticated relationship to traditional scenes of work amended by close observation of contemporary practices. Amman's originality lies less in the individuality of any given picture than in the patient recording and knowledgeable research shown in composing the first modern corpus of independent craft genre scenes.

Trade and craft paintings were already known in antiquity: many examples survive although mostly on decorated utensils. In his chapter of the *Historia Naturalis* devoted to ancient painting, Pliny the Elder gives an account of Peiraikos, the master of small scenes of daily life who "by his choice of a humble line perhaps marred his own success, however winning the highest glory that it had to bring; he painted barbers' shops, cobblers' stalls, asses, foodstuffs and similar subjects, earning for himself the name of ῥυπαρογράφος [*ruparographos*, i.e. painter of odds and ends]."[35] The two branches of painting attributed to Peiraikos, the scenes of craftsmen's shops and displays of foodstuffs, emerged again in Amman's generation as the independent genre scene and the still-life painting. At first, in the Antwerp circle of Pieter Aertsen, both were combined in a single painting and glossed with a nominal religious theme. By the end of the century both genre and still-life subjects were frequently painted as distinct picture types, given only a minimum of disguised symbolism. As the moral purpose of the *Ständebuch* is shifted to the text, and is there only suggested by implication, Amman's suite stands as an early example of the pure genre picture, instructive about its own subject, which is also the source of its aesthetic enjoyment.

Certain scenes of mundane labor did appear regularly in medieval art, but fixed in a theological context. The antique practice of illustrating the calendar with scenes of the labors pertinent to each month was easily joined to liturgical usage and continued as a part of the sculptural program on the portals of many cathedrals or as a preface to the more elaborate Books of Hours. Yet in even the most elegantly realistic miniatures in fifteenth-century calendars, such as the *Très Riches Heures* of Jean, Duke of Berry, the Grimani Breviary or the *Hortulus Animae,* each scene set beneath its corresponding zodiac sign remained essentially rustic, tracing the year in occupations which were intimately seasonal for the landed. The related but more restricted cycle of the seven *Children of the Planets* gathers the crafts and arts under the sign of Mercury, but as expressions of temperament and humor and not as individual presentations. There are several episodes in both Testaments which were usually accompanied by scenes of work, such as the first labors of Adam and Eve or the building of the Tower of Babel, while occasionally Catholic allegories were presented as genre scenes: the six women representing the *vita activa* on the voussoirs of the left doorway, north portal, at Chartres (c. 1225) are shown working at successive steps in the processing of wool. Some hagiographic themes also inspired quite detailed descriptions of daily work, such as St. Luke painting the Virgin or St. Crispinian as the patron saint of shoemakers working at a last.[36] Two outstanding instances of the fifteenth-century facility for absorbing religious content into an intensely real scene are Robert Campin's right wing of the *Mérode Altarpiece* (New York, Metropolitan Museum, The Cloisters) showing Joseph in his carpenter's shop, and Petrus Christus' portrait of a goldsmith in his studio (with his daughter and son-in-law) in the

Mercurius.

Fig. 15. Hans Sebald Beham, *The Children of the Planet Mercury.*
Woodcut, Pauli 909, before 1531.

guise of his patron saint Eloy (New York, Lehman Collection). In both a craft genre scene was instrumental in narrating a religious content, to which its purpose as a realistic depiction is inextricably wed.[37]

Secular scenes of craft and trade, sometimes based upon the same prototypes as the religious versions, appeared by the thirteenth century in donor portraits of guild members, as at Chartres; they are illustrated in a fourteenth-century technical manual, the Ypres *Book of Trades* (destroyed in World War I) which was largely devoted to the wool industry.[38] By the fifteenth century some work scenes were common enough as independent motifs to appear on playing cards: a tailor, woman potter and a barber-surgeon were used, as a single example, in a mid-fifteenth-century deck in Vienna (Kunsthistorisches Museum).[39] A close connection between guild patronage and secular illustration was maintained during this period in both the manuscript and printed versions of guild regulations, usually decorated with scenes of professional life. A Bolognese statute book of about 1470 (Bologna, Museo Civico) containing the rules of the linen drapers and furniture makers (*Statuti della Società dei Drappieri e Bracciaioli*) has a full-page miniature showing the storage, tailoring and sale of cloth and clothing in the guild's market. A similar scene of a market street with tailor, barber-surgeon and apothecary-grocer stalls appears in a French manuscript of *c.* 1510 of the *Gouvernement des Princes* (Paris, Bibliothèque de l'Arsenal Ms.fr.5062, f.149v). Although vignettes in both miniatures are suggestive of some compositions in the *Ständebuch,* they were intended only as particulars of a composite view of the guild's activities. Isolated representations of work do appear in an early printed book of Parisian ordinances, *Les Ordonnances de la Prévosté des Marchands et Echevinage de la Ville de Paris* (1500/01), which set out the regulations of working procedure, quality of goods and conditions of sale for the licensed guilds (e.g. linen shops must wash and shrink a shirt once before offering it for sale!). Most of these ordinances were illustrated by one of twenty-five woodcuts (with thirty repetitions) that focused upon the individual labor of the wine importer, charcoal burner, timber hauler and others, making each a theme in itself.[40]

However, the most extensive cycle of craft scenes anterior to the *Ständebuch* was also created in Nuremberg. In 1388 the Mendel family, an old and patrician dynasty in the city, founded (upon the rules of the Carthusian order) an old-age home for twelve craftsmen; the foundation lasted until the nineteenth century. Starting in about 1425, and

Fig. 16. Bolognese Master, *Drapers' Guild-Mart*. Painted miniature, c. 1470, Bologna, Museo Civico. (Courtesy Alinari—Art Reference Bureau)

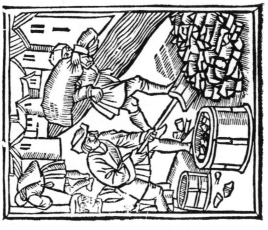
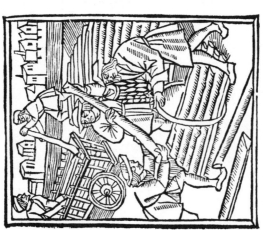

Figs. 17–19. Scenes of Trade: *Timber Haulers, Charcoal Burners and a Wine Merchant*. Woodcuts, 1500/01, from *Les Ordonnances ... de Paris*. (Courtesy The Pierpont Morgan Library)

continuing until 1549, the first volume of a three-part housebook was used as a necrology in which was entered a full-page portrait of each deceased member, shown engaged in his former trade. Despite some repetition, the almost 340 surviving pictures in this volume constitute a remarkable document of local craft technique; the high degree of accuracy in portraying the individual craftsman and his paraphernalia exceeds the rather mediocre quality of the art itself. As in the *Ständebuch*, settings are minimized abstractions, without real locale, standing for workshops and stalls. As in the *Ständebuch*, specific tools, wares and assorted implements are rendered with painstaking care. The Mendel housebook was not the source for Jost Amman's pictures: few compositions in either work reveal similarities that cannot be traced back to common models. Yet as a series of deliberate representations of individual workers and their crafts, the Mendel volume is the true parent of the *Ständebuch*, evincing a Nuremberg tradition from which Jost Amman's pictorial attitude was derived.[41]

In gathering, amending and amplifying a diffuse conglomeration of images Amman established a completely objective mode of picturing craft genre, free of contextual purpose other than the work itself. This is in marked contrast to both earlier religious and secular uses of genre scenes, and to contemporary low-life scenes, which, despite their probable antique origins, remained grotesque mimics of a limited range of social behavior.[42] Amman's pictures were intended as illustrations for a curious public, as an informative record of local customs, and as a visual adjunct to a text which primarily encouraged the Protestant work ethic. They were not caricatures or vulgarizations, but semi-scientific documentation combining several old and serious methods of viewing daily labor. They thus isolated the work scene as an autonomous branch of art, and gave it a new purpose as an independent subject. They act as a turning point between the religious genre of Pieter Aertsen, or the low-life scenes of the Flemish and Italian satiric painters and popular printmakers, and the sober, realistic genre painting of the Carracci and their followers. By the beginning of the next century new cycles of trade and craft illustrations began to appear: in c. 1600 Theodore Galle engraved twenty drawings by Stradanus which included, as *Nova Reperta* (New Inventions), printing, silk making and an astronomer's observatory.[43] In 1635 the Leiden etcher Jan Joris van der Vliet, who had worked with Rembrandt in 1631, issued a set of eighteen prints of small shop and cottage labor such as hat making, broom tying and the ubiquitous cobbler and wood turner.[44]

Figs. 20–25. Nuremberg Masters, *Workers in the Mendel Housebook: A Turner,* f.18v, *c.* 1425; *A Butcher,* f.59v, *c.* 1436; *A Cabinetmaker,* f.66v, *c.* 1444; *A Reliquary Maker,* f.79v, *c.* 1458; *A Nail Maker,* f.144v, *c.* 1529; *A Shoemaker,* f.146r, *c.* 1531. Painted miniatures, Nuremberg, Stadtarchiv. (Courtesy Hauptamt für Hochbauwesen, Nuremberg)

These rather archaic pictures suggest an earlier prototype, such as the Mendel manuscript, or prints of Amman's generation. Finally, at the end of the seventeenth century, Christoph Weigel published the *Abbildung der Gemein-Nützlichen Haupt-Stände* (Regensburg, 1698) with etched plates based on Amman's woodcuts. The large number of seventeenth-century Dutch paintings and prints of handworkers and tradespeople established this genre as a basic mode in Protestant iconography, extending to individual paintings and prints the observant attitude and moral heritage of the *Ständebuch* corpus. Thus Amman was instrumental in the creation of the modern genre subject, giving an artistic format to a traditional and yet evolving body of ideas about the purposes of man and the study of his environment. For the curious viewer to whom the world provides a source of constant instruction and profound joy, the *Ständebuch* was and remains an open window from "a warm study or parlour, without peril of the sea or danger of long and painful journeys."

Fig. 26. Jan Joris van der Vliet, *A Wood Turner*. Etching, 1635, R.46, Berlin, Kupferstichkabinett. (Courtesy Staatliche Museen Preussischer Kulturbesitz)

VII: EDITIONS OF THE STÄNDEBUCH

This Dover edition of the *Eygentliche Beschreibung Aller Stände auff Erden* completely reproduces the original German version of Hans Sachs, with 114 woodcuts by and after Jost Amman, and published in 1568 by Sigmund Feyerabend in Frankfurt at the press of Georg Raben. In the same year a Latin edition was published by Feyerabend with a text by Hartmann Schoper under the title: ΠΑΝΟΠΛΙΑ, *OMNIUM ILLIBERALIUM MECHANICARUM AUT SEDENTAriarum artium genera continens*, etc.; it was expanded by the introduction of eighteen woodcuts of military ranks used by Amman in other works, bringing the total number of prints to 132. Two cuts used in the German edition are replaced in the Latin: the organist, Plate 105, with a philosopher, and the kettledrummer, Plate 109, with the Emperor. The order of plates is also different, although in both editions the blocks were printed only on the recto side. Further editions of the German text, now amplified with 132 cuts, and the Latin, simultaneously appeared in 1574; many of the woodcuts appeared subsequently in the following books:

1. Wolf, *Lectionum memorabilium et reconditarum libri* XVI. 2 vols., Lauingen, 1600. fol.
2. *Caji Plinii Secundi des Weitberumbten Hochgelehrten alten Philosophi und Naturkündigers*, etc. (Pliny's *Natural History*), Frankfurt, 1618. 4to.
3. *PIAZZA UNIVERSALE: Das ist: Allgemeiner Schawplatz, Marckt und Zusammenkunfft aller Professionen*, etc. Frankfurt (Merian), 1641 and 1649. 4to.

A complete description of the differences between editions can be found in A. Andresen, *Der Deutsche Peintre-Graveur*, etc., I, Leipzig, 1864, p. 379 f., No. 231. See also C. Fairfax Murray, *Catalogue of a Collection of Early German Books in the Library of C. F. M.*, London, 1913, *s.v.*

New York   *Benjamin A. Rifkin*
29 September 1971

NOTES

1. The translations are from C. Headlam, *The Story of Nuremberg,* London, 1927. A more accurate account of Nuremberg's history and trade in the six-teenth century is found in W. Treue and R. Kellermann, "Die soziale und wirtschaftliche Bedeutung des Nürnberger Handwerks im 15. und 16. Jahr-hundert," *Das Hausbuch der Mendelschen Zwölfbrüderstiftung zu Nürnberg,* Munich, 1965, I, 71 ff. (cf. note 41).

2. L. Thorndike, *A History of Magic and Experimental Science,* II, New York, 1923, 401 ff.; A. M. Hind, *An Introduction to a History of Woodcut,* New York, 1935 (Dover reprint, 1963), 575 ff., 604 ff., 620, and 726 ff.; P. Durrieu, *La Miniature Flamande au Temps de la Cour de Bourgogne,* Paris-Brussels, 1927 (2nd ed.), 77.

3. C. H. Haskins, *Studies in Medieval Culture,* Cambridge, Mass., 1929, 25f. and 65.

4. Cf. E. H. Zeydel, *The Ship of Fools by Sebastian Brant,* New York, 1944 (Dover reprint, 1962), 21 ff., 24 ff., 31 ff. on translations and adaptations; cf. also A. Pompen, *The English Versions of the Ship of Fools,* London, 1925, *passim.*

5. F. Saxl, "Illustrated Pamphlets of the Reformation," *Lectures,* London, 1957, I, 255 ff.

6. Cf. L. B. Wright, *Middle-Class Culture in Elizabethan England,* Chapel Hill, 1935, 43 ff., 121 ff., and *passim* for a thorough examination of the "Protest-ant ethic" in English popular literacy, quite comparable to the German.

7. Thorndike, *op. cit.,* V, 139 ff.

8. For the three authors of 1542/3 and the *Peregrinationes* cf. the brief but useful exhibition catalogue *Renaissance Books of Science from the Collection of Albert E. Lownes,* ed. D. R. Godine, Dartmouth College, Hanover, 1970. I owe this *vade mecum* to the generosity of my friend Prof. Franklin Robinson. For the Coeck van Aelst cf. G. Marlier, *La Renaissance Flamande: Pierre Coeck d'Alost,* Brussels, 1966, 55 ff.

9. Sir Thomas Elyot, *The Book named the Governor,* ed. S. E. Lehmberg, London, 1962, 35.

10. Cf. P. O. Kristeller, "The Modern System of the Arts," *Renaissance Thought* II, New York, 1965, 163 ff., 178 ff.

11. For Varro see F. della Corte, *Enciclopedisti Latini,* Genoa, 1946, *passim,* and 33 ff. For Pliny cf. the critical analysis of the *Historia* in W. S. Teuffel, *History of Roman Literature,* edd. Schwabe and Warr, London, 1892, II, 95 ff., par. 312–3: F. Saxl, "Illustrated Medieval Encyclopedias," I & II, *op. cit.,* 228 ff. and 242 ff. Feyerabend's edition of Pliny appeared as Plinius Secundus, *Bücher von der Natur, art und eigentschafft der Creaturen Gottes,* tr. by J. Heyden, Frankfurt, 1565. A copy of this edition is in the Harvard rare book room and another is at Ann Arbor; the second edition of 1584 is at Yale, but its woodcuts have been changed. The first edition shows only a few common scenes of work, and with different cuts than the *Ständebuch.* I must thank Miss Helen

Zolas at the Library of Congress and Miss Jill Karhan at Harvard Library for help with a troublesome set of questions.

12. A. C. Crombie, *Medieval and Early Modern Science*, Garden City, 1959, I, 175 ff. and 179 f. For Hugo cf. Thorndike, *op. cit.*, II, 9 ff. with further literature.

13. The general relationship between Chartres' program and the *Speculum* of Vincent of Beauvais was first pointed out by E. Mâle, *L'Art Religieux du XIII*e *Siècle en France*, Paris, 1948 (8th ed.), 63 ff. Mâle's theory now needs some modification, although it is principally correct. Cf. on Chartres' windows A. Bulteau, *Monographie de la Cathédrale de Chartres*, Chartres, 1887–1901, I, 127 and III, 204 ff. and 242 ff. For Vincent cf. R. van Marle, *Iconographie de l'Art Profane au Moyen-Age et à la Renaissance*, The Hague, 1932, II, 252 ff.; Thorndike, *op. cit.*, II, 457 ff. with further literature.

14. For the style and dating of the reliefs cf. I. Toesca, *Andrea e Nino Pisano*, Florence, 1950, 28 ff. For Giovanni da San Gimignano cf. A. C. Crombie, *op. cit.*, 177. A series of relief panels showing various handworkers, e.g. cobbler, linen merchant, armorer, which are roughly analogous to the Chartres scenes and also date from the thirteenth century, are found in the cathedral of Piacenza in northern Italy; see G. de Francovich, *Benedetto Antelami*, Milan-Florence, 1952.

15. A. M. Hind, *op. cit.*, 291 f., 602 and 741: F. Klemm, "Die sieben mechanischen Kunste des Mittelalters," *Die BASF* XII/2, 1962, 48.

16. Cf. G. R. Owst, *Literature and Pulpit in Medieval England*, Oxford, 1961 (2nd ed.), 548 ff. and 553 f. and 554 n. 1.

17. C. T. Rapp, *Burgher and Peasant in the Works of Thomasin von Zirclaria, Freidank, and Hugo von Trimberg*, Washington, D.C., 1936, 64 ff., 102 ff. and 87 ff. for the text translated: *Diu kunst aber zwên wege hât: Der eine die sêle gain got ûf rihtet,/ Der ander des lîbes nôtdurft berihtet:/ Gelêrte liute ûf dem êrsten stênt,/ Hantwercliute den andern gênt;/ Der êrste büezet unverstandenheit,/ Der ander büezet kummers leit* (ll. 16066 ff.).

18. In Dürer's letters from Venice, 1506, and later in his diary of the trip to the Netherlands, 1520, three virtues are constantly recommended: thrift, pride in craft and modest, gentle behavior.

19. Originally published in *c.* 1509, the 1528 edition of this cant dictionary had Luther's famous preface. Cf. D. B. Thomas, *The Book of Vagabonds and Beggars*, etc., London, 1932, 1 ff.; on vagabond and mendicant satires in general cf. J. A. S. McPeek, *The Black Book of Knaves and Unthrifts*, Storrs, Connecticut, 1969, 30 ff.

20. C. H. Bell, *Peasant Life in Old German Epics*, New York, 1931, 3 ff.

21. C. T. Rapp, *op. cit.*, 65. Both bird comparisons are from Juvenal's satires.

22. The phrase "beatification of work" is derived from Mâle, *op. cit.*

23. D. MacGibbon, *Jean Bourdichon*, Glasgow, 1933, 82.

24. Anon., *Le Livre du Chastel de Labour par Jean Bruyant. A description of an Illuminated Manuscript of the fifteenth century, belonging to P. A. B. Widener, Philadelphia*, privately printed, 1909; this work contains an excellent synopsis and study of the poem. There is a facsimile of the Wynkyn de Worde printing of Alexander Barclay's translation of 1506 edited for the Roxburghe

Club by A. W. Pollard, Edinburgh, 1905. For the edition of Pigouchet for Vostre, Paris, 1499, cf. A. Blum, *Les Origines du Livre à Gravure en France*, Paris-Brussels, 1928, 39 f. For the *Ménagier de Paris* cf. E. Power, *The Goodman of Paris*, London, 1928; for Piers Plowman, cf. R. W. Frank, *Piers Plowman and the Scheme of Salvation*, New Haven, 1957.

25. On Theophilus cf. J. G. Hawthorne and C. S. Smith, *On Diverse Arts: The Treatise of Theophilus*, Chicago, 1963; on Villard de Honnecourt cf. T. Bowie, *The Sketchbook of Villard de Honnecourt*, Bloomington-London, 1959; for the small treatises and "Kunstbüchlin" type cf. E. Darmstaeder, *Berg-, Probier- und Kunstbüchlein*, 1926; for Biringuccio cf. *The Pirotechnia of Vannuccio Biringuccio*, ed. and tr. by S. C. Smith and M. T. Gnudi (1942), Cambridge, Mass., 1966 (4th ed.); for Agricola cf. H. C. and L. Hoover, Georgius Agricola, *De Re Metallica*, New York, 1912 (Dover reprint, 1950); for the extensive illustrations of mining and glass manufacture in Bohemian sources there is a fairly useful corpus of plates with an erratic text by V. Husa et al., *Traditional Crafts and Skills: Life and Work in Medieval and Renaissance Times*, Prague-London, 1967; for Besson cf. Thorndike, *op. cit.*, V, 594 ff. Amman's importance to the history of technology is somewhat ill defined; in effect, it is not the specifics of any given illustration which are of greatest importance, for each of these devices had been and continued to be of general service from the Middle Ages to the industrial revolution; rather it is as a cycle of craft illustrations that Amman introduces a new aspect into the history of modern art and science; for this cf. *infra* and the standard histories of science and technology already cited.

26. The basic material for the biography of Amman is included in A. F. Amman, *Geschichte der Familie Amman von Zürich*, Zurich, 1911; to this must be added K. Pilz, "Jost Amman 1539–1591," *Mitteilungen des Vereins für Geschichte der Stadt Nürnberg*, XXXVII, 1940, 201–252. Amman's birth date is set by the recorded date of his baptism. That Asper was his first teacher is only one of several surmises; cf. E. Frölicher, *Die Porträtkunst Hans Holbeins des Jüngeren und ihr Einfluss auf die schweizerische Bildnismalerei im XVI. Jahrhundert*, Strassburg, 1909, 65, on Amman's handsome but problematic portrait of a scholar, dated 1565, in Basel. For further literature, cf. K. Oberhuber, *Die Kunst der Graphik IV: Zwischen Renaissance und Barock*, Vienna, Albertina, 1968, 141 ff. and *passim*.

27. F. Thöne, "Ein Bildnis des Glasmalers Hieronymus Lang und einige Beiträge zu seiner und seines Sohnes Daniel Tätigkeit," *Zeitschrift für schweizerische Archaeologie und Kunstgeschichte*, I/2, 1939, 32 ff. A drawing in the Albertina, now attributed to Lang, was formerly given to Jost Amman; cf. H. Tietze et al., *Beschreibender Katalog der Handzeichnungen ... Albertina IV: Die Zeichnungen der Deutschen Schulen*, Vienna, 1933, 48, No. 375.

28. Cf. Oberhuber, *op. cit.*, 139 ff. and *passim*.

29. A. Andresen, *Der Deutsche Peintre-Graveur*, I, Leipzig, 1864, 99 ff. Andresen's biography is based upon the work of Becker, published in 1854, but with an accurate catalogue of Amman's separate prints and book illustrations.

30. Joachim von Sandrart, *Teutsche Academie der Edlen Bau-, Bild- und Mahlerey-Künste*, ed. A. R. Peltzer, Munich, 1925, 104.

31. A. Werner, introduction to *293 Renaissance Woodcuts for Artists and*

Illustrators: Jost Amman's Kunstbüchlin, New York (Dover), 1968, vii; Dr. Werner kindly informs me that he drew his reference from A. F. Amman, *op. cit.* Amman's own book could not have differed much from the theories of proportion and schemata for drawing of Dürer, Beham, Schön and Lautensack; cf. E. H. Gombrich, *Art and Illusion*, New York, 1961 (2nd ed.), 157 ff.

32. J. Schlosser Magnino, *La Letteratura Artistica*, Florence, 1964 (3rd ed.), 480 and 490; W. Waetzoldt, *Deutsche Kunsthistoriker*, Berlin, 1965 (2nd ed.), 22 ff. For distinctions in the seventeenth century between the "vulgar" and "sublime" in art, cf. J. Emmens, *Rembrandt en de Regels van de Kunst*, Utrecht, 1968.

33. E. Panofsky, "Albrecht Dürer and Classical Antiquity," *Meaning in the Visual Arts*, Garden City, 1955, 276.

34. For the dished wheel cf. C. Singer et al., *A History of Technology*, II, London (Oxford), 1956, 552; for Amman as a medical illustrator cf. Robert Herrlinger, *History of Medical Illustration*, New York, 1970, 122 and note 10 for further literature; cf. also 152 note 24 for a drawing that Amman sent his brother-in-law in Zurich, showing a Siamese twin.

35. K. Jex-Blake and E. Sellers, *The Elder Pliny's Chapters on the History of Art*, London, 1896, 144/145. See also Note 41 below.

36. For the illustrated calendars cf. J. C. Webster, *The Labors of the Months*, Evanston-Chicago, 1938; V. Leroquais, *Les Livres d'Heures Manuscrits de la Bibliothèque Nationale*, I, Paris, 1927, iii ff.; for the Children of the Planets cf. F. Lippmann, *Die Sieben Planeten*, Berlin, 1895; for the Chartres figures cf. E. Houvet, *Cathédrale de Chartres: Portail Nord*, II, Celles (S. et M.), 1919, pl. 1 ff.; A. Katzenellenbogen, *The Sculptural Programs of Chartres Cathedral*, Baltimore, 1959, 74.

37. For the concept of "disguised symbolism" cf. E. Panofsky, "Jan van Eyck's Arnolfini Portrait," *Burlington Magazine*, LXIV, 1934, 117 ff., and amplified in *Early Netherlandish Painting*, Cambridge, Mass., 1953, I, 164 ff., 201 ff. and *passim*; for the *Mérode Altarpiece* cf. M. Schapiro, " 'Muscipula Diaboli,' the Symbolism of the Mérode Altarpiece," *Art Bulletin*, XXVII, 1945, 182 ff.; for the St. Eloy painting cf. H. C. Smith, *The Goldsmith and the Young Couple or the Legend of S. Eloy & S. Godeberta by Petrus Christus*, Temple Sheen Press (Private), 1915, and Panofsky, *Early Netherlandish Painting*, s.v.

38. Cf. A. L. Gutmann, "Cloth-Making in Flanders," *Ciba Review*, XIV, October 1938, *passim* for illustrations from the MS.

39. E. Hartmann von Franzenschuld, "Ein höfisches Kartenspiel des XV. Jahrhunderts," *Jahrbuch der Kunsthistorischen Sammlungen des Allerhöchsten Kaiserhauses*, I, 1883, 101 ff., and II, 96 ff.

40. Hind, *op. cit.*, II, 667 f.; there is a copy in the Morgan Library, New York, with a typescript description.

41. The entire first volume has been reprinted with excellent introduction and notes edited by W. Treue et al., *Das Hausbuch der Mendelschen Zwölfbrüderstiftung zu Nürnberg*, 2 vols., Munich, 1965; the detailed notes to the plates in this publication include a wealth of material for the trades found in the *Ständebuch* and ought to be consulted. Cf. further W. Schultheiss, "Das Haus-

buch des Mendelschen Zwölfbrüderhauses zu Nürnberg von 1388/1425–1549," *Mitteilungen des Vereins für Geschichte der Stadt Nürnberg,* LIV, 1966, 94 ff.

The origin of this curious form of commemorative funerary monument was probably the local presence of numerous antique grave stelae dedicated to artisans. On each of these a votive relief accurately portrayed the daily work of the deceased. Many medieval work illustrations can be traced back to these reliefs, common in Gaul and Germania as well as Italy, while the conceptual stimulus for the *Hausbuch* necrologue was probably a form of Renaissance imitation of an antique commemorative mode. Cf. M. Rostovtzeff, *The Social and Economic History of the Roman Empire,* Oxford, 1963 (3rd ed.), I, Plates 28, 30 and 39, with further notes and literature, particularly for the important group of artisan stelae found in Trier and Mainz.

42. For the relatively little-known scenes of low-life genre in the sixteenth century and for a detailed treatment of Annibale Carracci's genre paintings, particularly the *Butcher's Shop* at Christ Church, Oxford, cf. D. Posner, *Annibale Carracci: A Study in the Reform of Italian Painting around 1590,* London-New York, 1971, I, 9 ff. It may be suggested that the slain and opened ox in this painting, as in a number of Flemish and Dutch *Butcher Shop* or *Smoke House* scenes, has a specific iconography: cf. E. de Jongh, *Zinne- en minnebeelden in de schilderkunst van de zeventiende eeuw,* N.S.O.K. and Prins Bernhard Fonds, n.p., 1967, 86 ff.

43. F. W. H. Hollstein, *Dutch and Flemish Etchings, Engravings and Woodcuts 1450-1700,* Amsterdam, 1948 f., VII, 87: 410-430.

44. Cf. my forthcoming *Etchings of the Rembrandt School.* For further material concerning German and some other genre art, cf. P. Brandt, *Schaffende Arbeit und bildende Künste vom Mittelalter bis zur Gegenwart,* Leipzig, 1928; E. Mummenhoff, *Die Handwerker in der deutschen Vergangenheit,* Leipzig, 1901. The development of related genre forms in Italy is surveyed with further literature in D. Posner, *op. cit.*

Note on the Text
and the Translations

The text of the *Ständebuch* consists of a title page (page 1 of the present edition); a dedication by the publisher, Sigmund Feyerabend, to the celebrated Nuremberg goldsmith Wenzel Jamnitzer, with a portrait of Jamnitzer at age 59 (page 3); a foreword by Feyerabend, dated December 24, 1567, which is also a continuation of the dedication (pages 3–7); 114 poems by Hans Sachs to accompany the 114 woodcuts by Jost Amman (pages 9–122; each of these poems has eight lines, rhyming in couplets; in general, the lines are iambic, with four beats); a concluding 28-line poem by Sachs (pages 123 and 124) and the colophon (page 124).

The complete translation of the title follows:

> Exact description of all ranks on earth, high and low, spiritual and secular, of all arts, crafts and trades, etc., from the greatest to the smallest; also of their origin, invention and usages. By the far-renowned Hans Sachs most diligently described and put into German rhymes very useful and pleasurable to read, and also with artistic illustrations the like of which has never been seen before, printed for the honor and satisfaction of all the ranks included in this book and particularly for the use of all artists, such as painters, goldsmiths, etc. With the permission of the Holy Roman Emperor. Printed at Frankfurt am Main. 1568.

Feyerabend's foreword, which includes publicity for two other books of his, does not merit a full translation. He says, in brief, that it is unchristian to lose faith in God just because society exhibits such vast differences in rank and fortune, since this inequality is part of God's plan: if all men were equally well off, none would want to do the work that must be accomplished to keep the world running. All occupations are necessary to human society, and all men should be satisfied with their jobs. Finally, the invention of printing is singled out for special praise (Gutenberg's name appears in the form Hans Kuttenberger).

It has also been decided not to translate Sachs' 114 poems *in extenso*, since they are quite clumsy, full of "padding" and burdened with terms that would involve long explanations. Instead, a prose condensation of each one, containing all the essential thought and much of Sachs' phraseology, is provided at the foot of pages 9 through 122. As a sample of what these jingles might sound like in English, full translations of the first two, in the meter and rhyme scheme of the original, follow:

THE POPE:
On earth I hold within my hand
The highest spiritual command.
When heresy sows lies and doubt,
It is my task to root it out
In every place with diligence,
Using God's word as my defense,
So that throughout all Christendom
Faith shall be one and peace shall come.

THE CARDINALS:
True servants of the Roman See,
Obedient to the Pope are we,
Providing counsel wise and sane
To help His Holiness remain
The foremost leader of mankind;
And when he leaves this life behind,
Only a Cardinal can hope
To be successor to the Pope.

As a further sample, Sachs' 28-line concluding poem has also been translated in full; it will be found, together with a translation of the colophon, on page 125.

An alphabetical English list of the ranks and occupations contained within the *Ständebuch* will be found in the Index on page 127.

Eygentliche Beschreibung

Aller Stånde auff Er=
den / Hoher vnd Nidriger / Geistlicher
vnd Weltlicher / Aller Künsten / Handwercken
vnd Handeln / ꝛc. vom grösten biß zum kleinesten /
Auch von jrem Vrsprung / Erfindung vnd
gebreuchen.

Durch den weitberümpten Hans Sachsen

Gantz fleissig beschrieben / vnd in Teutsche Reimen ge=
fasset / Sehr nutzbarlich vnd lustig zu lesen / vnd auch mit künstreichen
Figuren / deren gleichen zuvor niemands gesehen / allen Standen
so in diesem Buch begriffen / zu ehren vnd wolgefallen / Allen
Künstlern aber / als Malern / Goldschmiden / ꝛc.
zu sonderlichem dienst in Druck
verfertigt.

Mit Röm. Keys. Maiest. Freyheit.

Gedruckt zu Franckfurt am Mayn.

M. D. LXVIII.

1

Dem Ehrngeachten/

weitberümpten vnd Kunstreichen/
Wentzel Gommitzer/Goldschmidt vnd Bür-
gern zu Nürnberg/ꝛc. Meinem besondern vnd
Großgünstigen Herrn vnd guten freundt/ Wünsche ich
Sigmund Feyerabend/ Glück/Heil/vnd
ewige Seligkeit.

An findet/meines erachtens/viel/ auch wol bey
denen die sich Christen rhümen/ Gottlose Menschen/wel-
che/ wenn sie ernstlich bey sich bewegen/ vnd im hertzen
betrachten/wie sich so seltzame vnd wunderbarliche ver-
änderung in allen Ständen Menschlichs Geschlechts/
vom höchsten biß auff den Nidersten täglich on vnter-
laß zutragen/daß sie bey nahe in solche vngöttliche zweiffelung gerah-
ten/

)(ij

ten/als ob auch ein Gott im Himmel sey. Ja wenn sie sehen/ vnd sich in
den Chronicken erkündigen/ wie die grossen vnd gewaltigen König-
reich/ Fürstenthumb/ vnd andere Herrschafften/ plötzlich in einem au-
genblick steigen vnd zunemmen/ bald widerumb vnversehens zu schei-
tern vnd zu grundt gehen: Vnd daß die Gottlosen sampt den frommen
on allen vnterscheid dahin fallen/ vnd gleicher weise deß tods seyn/
dürffen sie noch vnverschempter herauß fahren/ vnd nach jrer tollen
vernunfft darauff schliessen/ Ob schon ein Gott im Himmel were/ müß-
ten sie doch zweiffeln/ ob er sich auch der Menschen/ jres Lebens/ anne-
me vnd jrer achte/ oder aber alle ding vnd Menschliche handlung/ on
Gottes vorwissen/ auß natürlichen vrsachen/ vnd on alle gefehr/ regiert
würden. Wie denn auch der Gottloß vnd schendliche Heyde Epicurus
bekennet hat/ es sey zwar ein Gott/ der gebe aber niemand nichts/ thue
auch niemands nichts zu dienst/ vnd lasse sich vmb nichts bekümmern.
Denn/ sagen sie (verstehe deß Epicuri anhang/ vnd die rohen sichern
Lestermeuler) warumb hat Gott/ dieweil er Allmechtig ist/ disem vnd
andern/ so in grossem armut von trübsal jr leben verschleissen/ nit auch
wie jenen/ die in allerley pracht vnd zeitlichem Reichthumb schweben/
ein so gut vnd treffliche narung bescheret? Vnd brauchen der schnöden
Gotteslesterung vil mehr/ welche meines fürhabens nicht seind allhie
zu erzehlen. Vñ seind also vil Abgöttische meinung/ auch fürnemlich bey
den alten philosophis entsprungen. Diese zwen/ Cleantes vnd Anaxi-
menes/ haben gesetzt/ die Lufft solte ein Gott seyn/ welchen auch der
Heidnisch poet Virgilius beyfellt/ wie im andern Buch Georgicorū zu
sehen. Xenocrates aber hat vermeinet/ es seyen der Götter achte. An-
dere/ vnd derselbigen nicht eine geringe anzal/ haben auß blindheit
öffentlich gelehret/ entweders sie wissen gar nichts drumb/ daß Götter
seyn solten/ oder die Götter gantz vnd gar verleugnet/ vnter welchen
auch gewesen Diagoras Atheos/ vnd Theodorus Cyrenaicus. Diese
aber alle/ wie niemand verneinen kan/ sind arme Heyden gewesen/ vñ
die warhafftige Gottes erkenntniß/ noch die Offenbarung seines heyligen Worts/ nicht gehabt/ sondern haben alles nach jrer vernunfft (die
zwar in allen Menschen verfinstert vnd geschwecht) geschlossen vnd ge-
glaubet. Daß man aber bey vns Christen/ die wir/ Gott lob/ Gottes er-
kenntniß/ seinen willen vnd barmhertzigkeit in seinem heyligen Wort
offenbaret/ klärlich begriffen haben/ noch so verfluchte vnd Gottlose
Menschen findet/ ist zu erbarmen/ vnd Gottes eyngeborner Son Jhe-
sus Christus/ welcher vmb vnsert willen auff die Welt komen ist/ wirt
am tag der Todten aufferstehung ein schweres vrtheil vber dieselbige
verächter vnd Epicurische Seuw fellen.

Daß aber nur allein ein Gott sey/ der warhafftig/ gerecht/ allmech-
tig/ vnd der sich der Menschen auff Erden gnädiglich annemme/ vnd

sonst alle ding mit Gottes allmächtigen vorwissen/ vnd nicht zufall=
weise/ wie jene fälschlich fürgeben/ regiert vnd ordiniert werden / wirdt
vns in seinem heyligen Wort vnd wunderbarlichen Creaturen gnug=
sam bezeuget. Als da seind/ das schöne vnd herrliche Gebeuw der gan=
tzen Welt/ die wunderbarliche Structur deß Himmels/ die liebe Sonn/
der helle Mond/ die liebliche vnd leuchtende Sterne/ vnd daß dieselbi=
gen alle/ Sonn/ Mond vnd Stern/ durch ein gewissen Motum oder be=
wegung für vnd für regiert werden/ daß zu geordneter vnd gewisser
zeit Tag wirdt/ vnd gleichfalls die Nacht nach bestimpter ordnung
eynfellt/ daß zu gebürlicher vnd seiner zeit Sommer vnd Winter wirt/ etc.

Vnd ich muß von dem Menschen auch etwas meldung thun/ daß
derselbig erstlich von Gott durch gebürliche mittel so wunderbarlich
geschaffen/ vnd folgends erhalten wirt/ vnd daß er kan/ vermittelst
Göttlicher gnad vnd hülff/ so vnterschiedlich reden/ vnd nach seiner not=
turfft außsprechen/ Also daß sein Rede kan vernommen werden/
vnd vber das in seinem gemüt/ beyde recht vnd vnrecht/ von einander
zu scheiden weiß/ vnd dergleichen vil mehr.

Wenn ich wölte weitläuffiger nach der lenge anzeigen/ was mir
dises zu beweisen nötig seyn würde/ achte ich es würde zu lang/ vnd dem
günstigen Läser/ welcher dessen vngezweiffelt ein bessern bericht hat/
verdrüßlich seyn/ vnd ein mißfall bringen. Wiewol es nicht vnnötig
hierzu were/ daß ich mit Exempeln comprobierte vnd verstendigte/
Nemlich wie alle Creaturen/ alle Thier/ allerley Kreuter vnd gewächß/
ein jeglichs nach seiner art/ alle jar vernewert/ gemehret/ vnd fortge=
pflantzt wirt. Hiervon zu lesen findet man bey allen erfahrnen natür=
lichen Historien schreibern/ vnd in sonderheit bey dem fürtrefflichen
hochgelehrten Caio Plinio Secundo/ welchen ich denn auch dem Teut=
schen Leser zu nutz vnd frommen eigentlich hab verteutschen/ vnd An=
no 1565. in Truck verfertigen lassen.

Daß aber die vngleichheit ist in Menschlichen Sachen/ Händeln/
vnd anschlägen/ auff/ daß ich widerumb zu meinem fürhaben kommet
kan on Göttliche Providentz vnd willen nicht geschehen/ man kan jr
auch in Menschlicher Gesellschafft nicht entrahten. Denn man muß
not halben Reiche haben/ die den Armen handreichung vnd hülff be=
weisen/ so muß man widerumb auch Arme haben/ welche den Reichen
mit Handwercken/ vnd sonst zu arbeiten geschickt seyen. Denn wer wolt
onst allerley nutzbarliche vnd notwendige Arbeit/ dem Menschlichen
Geschlecht dienstlich/ vollbringen? Niemand zwar/ wo wir alle in glei=
chem Standt vnd Reichthumb lebeten. Man muß Hohe vnd gewaltige
Oberkeit haben/ vnter welcher Regiment/ schutz vnd schirm/ vns Gott
setzt hat/ wie das der Apostel Rom. 13. bezeugt. Man muß fürtreff=

)(iij   liche

5

liche vñd gelehrte Männer haben/durch welcher weißheit der Gemein
nutz vnd Stattregiment geherrscht vnd gehandthabt werde.

Auß hochdringender not muß man auch allerley nutzbarliche Hand
werck/Kunst vnd Gewerb haben / vnd die Menschlich Gesellschafft
kan derselbigen keines entrahten/wie das allen verstendigen bekennt-
licher ist/denn hiervon vil zu schreiben.

Auß disen vnd andern dergleichen vrsachen vil mehr/auch vielem
vnrath vorzukommen / muß ein solche vngleichheit (darvon wir dro-
ben gesagt) in Menschlichen Leben gewißlich seyn.

Derhalben sol ein jeglicher in seinem Stand/Beruff oder Hand-
werck/dareyn in Gott gesetzt/wol zu frieden seyn/vnd treuwlich darin-
nen fortfahren/in betrachtung/daß auch der geringste /vnd ärmeste
Mensch/er sey was Wesens/Wird/oder Standts er wölle/bey der
Göttlichen Maiestat nicht vergessen sey. Wie denn in disem Büchlin
von allen Ständen/hohen vnd Nidrigen/Geistlichen vnd Weltlichen/
Sachen (vermöge seines Innhalts) gründtliche vnd eygentliche beschreibung ist/als von Keyser/Königen/Bapst/ec. Von den Hochgelehrten vnd jren gewönlichen Gradibus,vnd freyen Künsten/von allerley Handwercken/vom grösten biß zum kleinesten/von anfang der
Welt her biß auff dise jetzige zeit / so in Menschlichem leben nötig vnd
gebreuchlich seind/sampt derselbigen vrsprung/erfindungen/vnd weiter gelegenheit. Vnd seind vorwar dise Historien von erfindung aller
ding/nicht allein lustig zu lesen / Sondern bringen auch nicht geringen
nutz vnd erfahrung. Ich wil allein Exempels weise gantz kurtz anzey-
gen/von wem die Buchstaben vnd die löbliche Kunst der Truckerey erfunden seyen/auff daß der günstig Leser vernemmen möge/was vnd
wie in diesem Büchlin/von allen dingen/Geistlichen vnd Weltlichen
Sachen/tractiert oder gehandelt werde. Die alten Historien aber be-
zeugen/daß Cadmus/etliche einer mit namen Mercurius/die Buchsta
ben erstlich erfunden hab/Wiewol hiervon ein grosser streit ist bey den
Gelehrten/welche solches andern auch/die in erfindung der Buchstaben jr bestes gethan/zueygnen. Es sey aber demselbigen wie jm wölle/
so ist es zwar ein vnaußsprechliche gutthat / Sintemal allein durch
schreibens Kunst(dazu Buchstaben nötig) der gedechtniß bestendig-
keit erhalten/vnd alle ding zu gedencken von nöten/von schaden deß
vergeß errettet werden/vnd vorzeiten/als man der Truckerey geman-
gelt/hat man alle Bücher abschreiben müssen/vnd ehe das Papyrma-
chen auffkommen/Dattel vnd Bircken Rinden hierzu gebraucht. Derhalben ist dasselbig wie Polydorus Vergilius spricht/den Menschen ein
grosse gab gewesen/aber keines wegs gegen diser zuvergleichen/so wir
zu diser zeit vberkommen haben. Denn so jetziger zeit ein neuwe Matery zu schreiben erfunden ist/wirt in einem tag so vil Schrifft von einem

nem Menschen gedruckt/als in etlichen Wochen von vilen geschrieben
möcht werden. Darauß so ein grosse menge der Bücher in allen Kün=
sten an tag kompt. Es seind auch mit diser löblichen Kunst behendig=
keit/Griechischer vnd Lateinischer Gelehrten/fürtreffende nutzbarkei=
ten vnd vnderweisungen/gleich so wol als in Teutscher Sprach/an vns
kommen/daß sie billich in hoher acht sol behalten werden. Mich dün=
cket aber auch zimlich/ den Erfinder diser löblichen Kunst/seines wol
angewendten fleisses nicht zu berauben/damit die nachkommen wissen/
von wem sie dise Göttliche gutthat empfangen haben/ vnd wem sie es
zurechnen sollen. Darumb hat Hans Kuttenberger/ auß Teutscher
Nation bürtig/ ein Mann von Ritterlichen Ehren/ am aller ersten in
der Statt Mentz/am Rhein gelegen/dise Kunst/Schrifften zu trucken/
erdacht/ vnd ist daselbst zu treiben angefangen/ auch ist nicht mit we=
niger geschickligkeit/der schwartzen Farben zubereitung/ welcher sich
jetzt die Buchdrücker gebrauchen/ von jm erfunden worden. Hiervon
mag gemeldten Authorem weiter lesen wem es gefellig. Vñ wirt fast in
allen stücken dise ordnung gehalten/daß benennt werde/ wer ein jegliche
Kunst vnd Handwerck erfunden/auch wo es erfunden/ wie denn dises
mein Büchlin/so bey nahe eben desselbigen Innhalts mit deß Polydori
Vergilÿ fein artiglich beschreibet/Welches ich nicht on geringen kosten
in eine verstendtliche vnd richtige ordnung habe bringen lassen/ vnd
auch mit künstreichen Figuren aller vnd jeder angeregten stück geziert/
allen Künstlern/ vnd menniglich zu sonderm wolgefallen/ nutz vnd
ehren/ in druck verfertigt/auch in kurtz vormittels Göttlicher gnaden/
alle Thier gleichßfalles in druck verfertigen vnd an tag geben wil.

Dieweil ich nun/ Großgünstiger Herr vnd guter Freundt/diß Büch=
lin Von erfindung aller ding/ nach gemeiñ brauch einem sonderlichen
der freyen vnd löblichen Künste Liebhabern/ habe dediciern vnd zu
schreiben wöllen/ Jr aber vor andern/obgedachter Künste Liebhaber
seyt/ bin ich vervrsacht/ euch als meinem sonder geliebten Großgünsti=
gen Herrn vnd Freund/gemeldtes Büchlin zu zuschreiben/ vnd damit
zu verehren/auff daß solcher gestalt vnd meinung euwer Name vnd
Geschlecht(welche on das berümpt seyen) menniglichen bekänntlicher/
vnd vnsterblich gemacht würde. Bitt derwegen/ jr wolt dasselbig zu
einem glückseligen Neuwen Jar/von mir freundtlich annemmen/ vnd
gefallen lassen. Hiermit seyt Gott dem Allmechtigen sampt den eu=
wern in seinen gnädigen schutz vñ schirm befohlen. Da=
tum Franckfurt am Mayn den 24. Decem-
bris/Anno 1 5 6 7.

Der Bapst.

Ich erhalte in meiner Hend/
Auff Erd das Geiſtlich Regiment.
Wo entſtehe Irrthumb vnd Ketzerey/
Daß ich das alls außreute frey/
Mit dem Heiligen Gottes Wort/
Mit hohem fleiß an allem ort/
Daß in der gantzen Chriſtenheit
Fried bleib in Glaubens Einigkeit.
                              B   Cardi-

THE POPE is the spiritual guide of men; he roots out heresy and strives
after peace through unity of faith.

Der Cardinal.

Wir sind Diener deß Stuls zu Rom/
Dem Bapst gantz treuw vnd gehorsam/
Mit weiß/fürsichtig Hülff vnd Raht/
Auff daß sein hohe Maiestat
Auff Erd der aller höchst besteh/
Vnd wenn er denn mit tod abgeh
Daß vnser einer werd zu letzt
In sein Bäpstlichen Stul gesetzt.

B ij   Der

THE CARDINALS are faithful counselors of the Pope, and his successor
will be chosen from among them.

Der Bischoff.

Ich bin gesatzt in diß Bistum/
Daß ich das Euangelium
Vnd Gottes Wort dem volck sol predgen/
Die sünding Gwissen tröstn vnd ledgen
Bannen die widerspänstig Rott/
Vnd den armen reichen das Brot/
Auff daß der Glaub vnd Gottes Ehr/
Sich in meiner Gmein wachß vnd mehr.

Die

THE BISHOP preaches the Gospel to the people, comforts sore con-
sciences, combats enemies of the faith and feeds the poor so that God
will be honored within his diocese.

Die Pfaffen.

Wir sind von dem Bischoff erwehlt
Vnd der Christlich Gmein fürgestellt
Sie zu vnterrichtn vnd lehren
Mit Gottes Wort/ sich zubekehrn
Von Sünden/wo sie gfallen sent
Vnd jn reichen die Sacrament/
Den Leib Christi/Tauff vnd die Buß·
Wie vns klar vnderricht Paulus.

Münich

THE PRIESTS are chosen by the bishop to turn their congregations from sinning ways and to give them the sacraments as St. Paul instructed.

Die Münch.

Wir Münich vor vralten jarn
Einsidel vnd Waldbrüder warn/
Lagen in andechting Gebett/
Mit fasten wachen/frü vñd spet/
Hofften dardurch selig zu werdn/
Doch lebn wir jetzt anderß auff Erdn/
Mancherley Orden/ Rott vnd Sect
Da nicht viel Geistes innen steckt.

               C   Jacobæ

THE MONKS long ago were hermits and forest dwellers who constantly prayed and fasted, hoping for salvation, but nowadays they belong to a variety of orders and sects that are not particularly spiritual.

Die Jacobs Brüder.

Wir Jacobs brüder mit grossem hauffen
Im Land sind hin vnd her gelauffen/
Von Sanct Jacob/Ach vnd gen Rom
Singen vnd bettlen one schom/
Gleich anderen presthafften armen/
Offt thut vns der Bettel Stab erwarmen
In Händen/alsdenn wir es treibn
Vnser lebtag faul Bettler bleibn.

C ij   Der

THE PILGRIMS, or "Brothers of St. James," are hordes of lazy singing
beggars who swarm shamelessly over the countryside.

Der Keyſer.

Römiſch Keyſerlich Maieſtat
Helt mit ſein Fürſten weiſen Raht/
Wie er mit Keyſerlichem gwalt
Das Römiſch Reich ſchütz vnd erhalt/
Vnd aller Vngrechtigkeit wehr/
Dardurch erlang ruhm / preiß vnd ehr/
Wie Keyſer Julius Ceſar/
Welcher der erſte Keyſer war.

C iij   Der

THE HOLY ROMAN EMPEROR takes counsel with the Princes to ensure
justice and the welfare of the Empire, thus acquiring fame like the first
Caesar, Julius.

Der König.

Römisch Königlich Maiestat gut/
Die vnghorsamen straffen thut/
Vnd erhelt fried im gantzen Land/
Mit siegreicher vnd starcker hand/
Am Türckn vnd andren Tyrannen
Wo die auffwerffn jrn Streitfahnen/
Die stürtzt er vnter diß Römisch joch/
Wie Romulus der König hoch.

Der

THE KING ("Roman King," i.e. king of Germany, son of the Emperor) chastises the disobedient and keeps peace in the land, forcing the Turks and other tyrants under the yoke like the first Roman king, Romulus.

Der Fürst.

Der ift ein recht löblicher Fürft
Den nach der Gerechtigfeit dürft/
Der fein vnderthon thut alls guts
Helt in vätterlichn treuwen fchutz/
Vnd helt all Straß im Land fauber
Vnd tilgt auß die Mördr vnd Rauber
Die Land vnd Leut verderben fehr/
Der Fürft erzeigt fein Fürftlich ehr.
D   Der

THE PRINCE (of the Empire) thirsts for justice and his subjects' well-being, keeps the roads safe and exterminates dangerous criminals.

Der Gentelon.

Ich bin ein edler Gentelon
Ein gwaltig/reich/herrlicher Mann/
Jederman ein auffsehen hat
Auff mein geberde/weiß vnd that/
Derhalb steh ich in starckem hoffn
Das Regiment sich mir noch offn/
Daß ich zum Hertzog werd erwehlt
Vnd der gwalt in mein händ gestellt.

D ij   Der

THE NOBLEMAN is rich, powerful and looked up to; he hopes to be made
a duke.

Der Doctor.

Ich bin ein Doctor der Artzney/
An dem Harn kan ich sehen frey
Was kranckheit ein Menschn thut beladn
Dem kan ich helffen mit Gotts gnadn
Durch ein Syrup oder Recept
Das seiner kranckheit widerstrebt/
Daß der Mensch wider werd gesund/
Arabo die Artzney erfund.

                    D iij   Der

Der Apotecker.

Ich hab in meiner Apoteckn
Viel Matery die lieblich schmeckn/
Zucker mit Würtzen ich conficier
Mach auch Purgatzen vnd Clistier/
Auch zu stercken den krancken schwachn
Kan ich mancherley Labung machn/
Das alles nach der Artzte raht
Der seinen Brunn gesehen hat.

Der

THE PHARMACIST sells tasty confections, prepares purges and enemas, and fills doctors' prescriptions.

Der Astronomus.

So bin ich ein Astronomus/
Erkenn zukünfftig Finsternuß/
An Sonn vnd Mond/durch das Gestirn
Darauß kan ich denn practiciern/
Ob künfftig komm ein fruchtbar jar
Oder Theuwrung vnd Kriegßgefahr/
Vnd sonst manicherley Kranckheit/
Milesius den anfang geit.

                                E   Der

THE ASTRONOMER predicts eclipses and tells by the stars whether the year will be fruitful or one of dearth, war and disease; Milesius was the first astronomer.

Der Procurator.

Ich procurir vor dem Gericht/
Vnd offt ein böse sach versicht/
Durch Loic falsche list vnd renck
Durch auffzug auffsatz vnd einflenck/
Darmit ichs Recht auffziehen thu:
Schlecht aber zuletzt vnglück zu
Daß mein Parthey ligt vnterm gaul
Hab ich doch offt gfüllt beutl vnd maul.

E ij   Der

THE LAWYER often defends an unjust cause in court, using shrewd ploys
and obtaining delays; if his client loses, the lawyer has still filled his
own purse.

Der Schrifftgiesser.

Ich geuß die Schrifft zu der Druckrey
Gemacht auß Wißmat/Zin vnd Bley/
Die kan ich auch gerecht justiern/
Die Buchstaben zusammn ordniern
Lateinisch vnd Teutscher Geschrifft
Was auch die Griechisch Sprach antrifft
Mit Versalen/ Puncten vnd Zügn
Daß sie zu der Truckrey sich fügen.

C iij   Der

THE TYPEFOUNDER casts type from bismuth, tin and lead: Roman,
Gothic and Greek alphabets, capital letters and punctuation marks.

Der Reiſſer.

Ich bin ein Reiſſer frü vnd ſpet/
Ich entwürff auff ein Linden Bret/
Bildnuß von Menſchen oder Thier/
Auch gewechß mancherley monier/
Geſchrifft/auch groß Verſal buchſtaben/
Hiſtorj / vnd was man wil haben/
Künſtlich/daß nit iſt außzuſprechen/
Auch kan ich diß in Kupffer ſtechen.

                                    Der

THE DRAFTSMAN, or designer, draws letters and pictures of all sorts on wood blocks most artistically; he can also engrave the pictures on copper.

Der Formschneider.

Ich bin ein Formen schneider gut/
Als was man mir für reissen thut/
Mit der federn auff ein form bret
Das schneid ich denn mit meim geret/
Wenn mans deñ druckt so find sich scharff
Die Bildnuß/wie sie der entwarff/
Die steht/denn druckt auff dem papyr/
Künstlich denn auß zustreichen schier.

F　　　Der

THE BLOCK CUTTER engraves onto the wood blocks the art that the draftsman has prepared; the printed image comes out as clear as the original drawing.

Der Papyrer.

Jch brauch Hadern zu meiner Mül
Dran treibt mirs Rad deß wassers viel/
Daß mir die zschnitn Hadern nelt/
Das zeug wirt in wasser einquelt/
Drauß mach ich Pogn/auff dē filtz bring/
Durch preß das wasser darauß zwing.
Denn henck ichs auff/laß drucken wern/
Schneweiß vnd glatt / so hat mans gern.

F ij   Der

THE PAPER MAKER, in his water-driven mill, makes smooth white sheets
of paper from rags that have been chopped up, soaked, placed on the
sieve, pressed and dried.

Der Buchdrücker.

Ich bin geschicket mit der preß
So ich aufftrag den Firniß reß/
So bald mein dienr den bengel zuckt/
So ist ein bogn papyrs gedruckt.
Da durch kombt manche Kunst an tag/
Die man leichtlich bekommen mag.
Vor zeiten hat man die bücher gschribn/
Zu Meintz die Kunst ward erstlich triebn.

THE BOOK PRINTER applies the ink, his aide pulls the lever and a sheet
is printed; thus many arts become readily accessible; books used to be
written by hand; printing was first practiced in Mainz.

Der Brieffmaler.

Ein Brieffmaler bin aber ich/
Mit dem Penfel so nehr ich mich/
An streich die bildwerck so da stehnd
Auff Papyr oder Pergament/
Mit farben/vnd verhöchs mit gold/
Den Patronen bin ich nit hold/
Darmit man schlechte arbeit macht/
Darvon auch gringen lohn empfacht.

Der

THE ILLUMINATOR colors and gilds pictures on paper or parchment;
he does not hold with stencils, which produce poor work that is less
highly remunerated.

Der Buchbinder.

Jch bind allerley Bücher ein/
Geiſtlich vnd Weltlich/groß vnd klein/
Jn Perment oder Bretter nur
Vnd beſchlags mit guter Clauſur
Vnd Spangen/vnd ſtempff ſie zur zier/
Jch ſie auch im anfang planier/
Etlich vergüld ich auff dem ſchnitt/
Da verdien ich viel geldes mit.

G   Der

THE BOOKBINDER binds large and small books on all subjects in parchment or planed boards which are fitted with clasps and ornamented;
some books are gilded on the edges.

Der Handmaler.

Die Kunst der perspectiff ich pur
Bericht bin/vnd Contrafactur/
Dem Menschen ich mit farb kan gebn
Sein gstalt/ als ob diß Bild thu lebn
Stätt/Schlösser/Wasser/Berg vñ Wäld/
Ein Heer/ sam lig ein Fürst zu Feld/
Kan ich so eigentlich anzeygn/
Als stehe es da Leibhafftig eign.

G ij   Der

THE PAINTER is skilled in perspective and the imitation of nature; he can make lifelike portraits and paint towns, castles, bodies of water, hills, woods and armies.

Der Glaſſer.

Ein Glaſſer war ich lange jar/
Gut Trinckgläſer hab ich fürwar/
Beyde zu Bier vnd auch zu Wein/
Auch Venediſch glaßſcheiben rein/
In die Kirchen/ vnd ſchönen Sal/
Auch rautengläſer allzumal/
Wer der bedarff/ thu hie einkern/
Der ſol von mir gefürdert wern.

G iij   Der

THE GLAZIER makes good wine and beer glasses and "Venetian" circular and diamond-shaped panes for churches and fine rooms.

Der Glaßmaler.

Einen Glaßmaler heiſt man mich/
Jn die Gläſſer kan ſchmeltzen ich/
Bildwerck / manch herrliche Perſon/
Adelich Frauwen vnde Mann/
Sampt jren Kindern abgebild/
Vnd jres gſchlechts Wappen vnd Schilt/
Daß man erkennen kan darbey/
Wann diß Geſchlecht herkommen ſey.

Der

THE GLASS PAINTER paints pictures of people and coats-of-arms of
noble families on glass.

Der Seydensticker.

Ich aber kan wol Seyden stickn/
Mit Gold die brüst vnd Ermel rückn/
Versetzet mit Edlem gestein/
Auch mach ich güldin Hauben rein/
Krentz vnd harband von perlein weiß/
Künstlich Mödel mit hohem fleiß/
Auch Kirchen grēht Meßgwant vnd Albn
Kan ich wol schmückn allenthalben.

H   Der

THE EMBROIDERER does silk embroidery, works gold and precious
stones into sleeves and breast pieces, makes caps, garlands and hair
ribbons with gold and pearls, and adorns ecclesiastical garments.

Der Goldtschmid.

Ich Goldtschmid mach köstliche ding/
Sigel vnd gülden petschafft Ring/
Köstlich geheng vnd Kleinot rein
Versetzet mit Edlem gestein/
Güldin Ketten/Halß vnd Arm band/
Scheuren vnd Becher mancher hand/
Auch von Silber Schüssel vnd Schaln/
Wer mirs gutwillig thut bezaln.

H ij   Der

THE GOLDSMITH makes valuable seals and signet rings, pendants and jewels set with precious stones, chains, necklaces, bracelets, goblets and silver platters and bowls.

Der Steinſchneider.

Ich aber ſchneyd Edelgeſtein
Auff meiner ſcheiben groß vnd klein/
Als Granat/ Rubin vnd Demut/
Schmarack/ Saphyr/ Jacinthn gut/
Auch Calcidonj vnd Perill/
Schneyd auch der Fürſten Wapen viel/
Die man ſetzt in die Pettſchafft Ring/
Sunſt auch viel Wappen aller ding.

H iij   Der.

THE GEM CUTTER cuts jewels on his wheel: garnets, rubies, diamonds, emeralds, sapphires, jacinths, chalcedony, beryl; he also cuts coats-of-arms for signet rings.

Der Bildhauwer.

Bildschnitzen so hab ich gelehrt/
Vor jaren war ich hoch geehrt/
Da ich der Heyden Götzen macht/
Die man anbett vnd Opffer bracht/
Die ich machet von Holtz vnd Stein/
Auch von Cristallen sauber rein/
Geliedmasirt vnd wolgestalt/
Die mit Gelt wurden hoch bezalt.

Der

THE SCULPTOR was highly regarded and well paid in antiquity, when
he made shapely idols of wood, stone and crystal.

Der Kauffmann.

Ich aber bin ein Handelsmann/
Hab mancherley Wahr bey mir stan/
Würtz/Arlas/Thuch/Wolln vñ Flachß.
Sammat/Seiden/Honig vnd Wachß/
Vnd ander Wahr hie vngenannt/
Die führ ich eyn vnd auß dem Land/
Mit grosser sorg vnd gfehrlichkeit
Wann mich auch offt das vnglück reit.

J   Der

THE MERCHANT deals in spices, various kinds of cloth, honey, wax and many other products which he imports and exports at great financial risk.

Der Jüd.

Bin nicht vmb sonst ein Jüd genannt/
Jch leih nur halb Gelt an ein Pfandt/
Löst mans nit zu gesetztem Ziel/
So gilt es mir dennoch so viel/
Darmit verderb ich den loßn hauffn/
Der nur wil Feyern / Fressn vnd Sauffn/
Doch nimpt mein Handel gar nit ab/
Weil ich meins gleich viel Brüder hab.

J ij   Der

THE JEW is rightly so named; he gives only half value for a pledged object which he keeps if not redeemed on time; he destroys many thoughtless carousers, but his business thrives.

Der Müntzmeister.

In meiner Müntz schlag ich gericht/
Gute Müntz an kern vnd gewicht/
Gülden/Cron/Taler vnd Bazen/
Mit gutem preg / künstlich zu schatzen/
Halb Bazen/Creutzer vnd Weißpfennig/
Vnd gut alt Thurnis / aller mennig
Zu gut/in recht guter Landswerung/
Dardurch niemand geschicht gferung.

J iij   Der

THE COIN STAMPER makes coins of all denominations of proper metal
content and weight, artistically stamped.

Der Goltschlager.

Silber/ Golt/ ich zu Blettern schlag/
Diß zu seim Handwerck brauchen mag/
Maler vnd Brieffmaler darbey/
Vnd ander Handwerck zur Malerey/
Auch mag man das Golt maln vnd reibn/
Ein Gülden Schrifft darmit zu schreybn/
Dergleich mag man Golt auch spinnen/
Wircken/ vnd vernehn mit sinnen.

Der

THE GOLD LEAF MAKER hammers gold thin for painters, illuminators and other artists; gold is also ground and rubbed into a writing material; it is also woven and sewn into textiles.

Der Krämer.

Ich bin ein Krämer lange jar/
Kompt/vnd kaufft hie mancherley Wahr/
Als Brüch/Pfeiffen/vnd Schlötterlein/
Item/Würtz/Zucker vnd Brentn Wein/
Spiegel/Schelln/Käm/nadl vñ Harbät/
Leckkuchn/Nestel vnd Brillen gnannt/
Die Krämerey mancherley Wahrn/
Erfand lieber Pater vor jarn.

                    K   Der

THE PEDDLER sells whistles and rattles, spices, sugar and brandy, mirrors, bells, combs, needles and hair ribbons, straps, eyeglasses and much more.

Der Beutler.

Hieher zu mir wer kauffen wil/
Hie find jr gmachter arbeit viel/
Hirschn/Semisch/Egrisch vñ Preuſſiſch/
Cöllſch / Schäffen / Kelbren vñ Reuſiſch/
Manns wetſchger gemacht allerhandt/
Auch Händtſchuch mancher art genannt/
Darzu Frauwen Beutel wolgſchaffn/
Auch für Beuwrlin/Münch vñ Pfaffen.

K ij   Der

THE BAG MAKER manufactures leather bags, pouches, purses and gloves
of many kinds for townspeople and for farmers, monks and priests.

Der Gürtler.

Hie find ir Gürtel wol gemacht
Von Läder/ artlich vnd geschlacht/
Von Rincken/Senckel/hübsch ergrabn/
Von Lauberck Meisterlich erhaben/
Gestempfft/glatt/breit vnd auch schmal/
Mannsgürtel auff das best zumal/
Mach auch stempffeyßn vnd Brenneysen/
Grab Sigel / wie ich kan beweißn.

K. iij   Der

THE BELT MAKER manufactures leather belts of all widths artistically punched and stamped; he also makes dies and branding irons and engraves seals.

Der Nestler.

Mein Nestl von gutem Läder gantz/
Beschlagen wol mit Farben glantz/
Rot/Braun/Gelb/Aschenfarb vñ Weiß/
Köllisch Nestel / vernitet mit fleiß/
Vngerisch Nestel/zeh/ lang vnd starck/
Gering Nestel auff den Jarmarck/
Auch der Schnür Riemen dreyerley/
Drumb wer jhr darff/ mach sich herbey.

Der

THE THONG MAKER manufactures painted leather thongs and straps
of various styles, qualities and colors.

Der Metzger.

Hieher/ wer Fleisch nit kan gerahten/
Zu Sieden / Kochen vnd zu Brahten/
Von Ochsen/ Kelber/ Schaffen.vñ schwein/
Gut / feist/ die frisch gestochen seyn/
Gut vorricht/ Kalbsköpff / Füß vnd Kröß/
Kuttelfleck / Ochsenmägen sind nit böß/
Welcher mir bar Gelt zelet auff/
Dem wil ich geben guten Kauff.

Der

THE BUTCHER sells freshly slaughtered beef, veal, mutton and pork,
calves' heads and feet, offal, tripes.

Der Jäger.

Ich bin meines Herrn Jäger worn/
Mit mein Hunden vnd Jägerhorn
Ich Bern vnd wild Schwein hetz/
Die Stich ich denn in meinem Netz/
Rehe/Hirschen/Füchß/Wölff vñ Haßn
Müssen die Heut hinder jn laßn/
Den ich nachspür/Wäld/Berg vñ Thal
Fell jr ein jar ein grosse zal.

C ij   Der

THE HUNTSMAN, a nobleman's servant, hunts bears, wild boars, deer,
foxes, wolves and hares in forests and over hill and dale.

Der Koch.

Ich bin ein Koch / für erbar Gest
Kan ich wol kochen auff das best/
Reiß/ Pfeffer / ander gut Gemüß/
Vögel/Fisch / Sültzen/reß vnd süß/
Für den Bauren vnd Handwercksmann/
Hirß/Gersten / Linsen / Erbeiß vnd Bon/
Rotseck/Würst/Suppen/Rübn vñ Kraut
Darmit sie auch füllen jr Haut.

Der

THE COOK prepares excellent rice, vegetables, fowl, fish and pickled food
for the gentry; for farmers and workers he makes millet, barley, lentils,
peas and beans, sausages, soups, turnips and cabbage. **47**

Der Müller.

Wer Korn vnd Weitz zu malen hat/
Der bring mirs in die Mül herab/
Denn schütt ichs zwischen den Mülstein
Vnd mal es sauber rein vnd klein/
Die Kleyen gib ich treuwlich zu/
Hirsch/Erbeiß/ich auch neuwen thu/
Dergleich thu ich auch Stockfisch bleuwn/
Würtz stoß ich auch mit gantzn treuwen .

Der

THE MILLER pours the grain brought to him between the millstones and grinds it, and does not withhold the bran; he also pounds stockfish and crushes herbs.

Der Beck.

Zu mir rein/wer hat Hungers not/
Ich hab gut Weiß vnd Rücken Brot/
Auß Korn/Weißen vnd Kern/bachen/
Gesaltzn recht/mit allen sachen/
Ein recht gewicht/das recht wol schmeck/
Seiñel/Bretzen/Laub/Spuln vñ Weck/
Dergleich Fladen vnd Eyerkuchn/
Thut man zu Ostern bey mir suchn.

                M   Der

THE BAKER makes fine breads from various flours, properly flavored
and of just weight, also rolls, pretzels and flat cakes and egg biscuits
for Eastertime.

Der Bauwer.

Ich aber bin von art ein Bauwr/
Mein Arbeit wirt mir schwer vnd sauwr/
Ich muß Ackern/Seen vnd Egn/
Schneyden/Mehen/ Heuwen dargegn/
Holtzen/vnd einführn Hew vnd Treyd/
Gült vñ Steuwr macht mir viel hertzleid
Trinck Wasser vnd iß grobes Brot/
Wie denn der Herr Adam gebot.

M ij   Der

THE FARMER works very hard ploughing, sowing, harrowing, cutting,
mowing, haymaking, woodgathering and harvesting; taxes plague him;
he lives on coarse bread and water.

Der Bierbreuwer.

Auß Gersten sied ich gutes Bier/
Feißt vnd Süß/ auch bitter monier/
In ein Breuwkessel weit vnd groß/
Darein ich denn den Hopffen stoß/
Laß den in Brennten külen baß/
Damit füll ich darnach die Faß
Wol gebunden vnd wol gebicht/
Denn giert er vnd ist zugericht.

M iij   Der

THE BREWER makes sweet and bitter beer from barley and hops in a
large vat; when cool, the beer is poured into solid casks in which it
ferments.

Der Weydmann.

Ich bin ein Weydmann ringer hand/
Beyde zu Wasser vnd zu Land/
Ich scheuß heimlich die Aurhanen/
Wenn sie faltzn auff hohen Tannen/
Die Ranger fach ich mit Falckn/
Die sie herab felln vnd walcken/
Antvögel vnd Wildgenß ich scheuß/
Meins Weydwercks ich offt wol geneuß.

Der

THE HUNTER, or fowler, shoots grouse and wild ducks and geese, and
catches herons with falcons.

Der Schneider.

Ich bin ein Schneider/mach ins Feld/
Den Krieges Fürsten jre Zelt/
Mach Reñdeck zu Stechn vnd Thurnier/
Auff Welsch vnd Frantzösisch Manier/
Kleid ich sie gantz höfflicher art/
Jr Hofgsind vnd die Frauwen zart/
Kleid ich in Sammet Seiden rein/
Vnd in wullen Thuch die Gemein.

N   Der

THE TAILOR makes military tents, cloth for jousts and tourneys, Italian and French style, garments of silk and satin for courtiers and ladies, of wool for commoners.

Der Kürschner.

Wol her/ich fütter Röck vnd Schaubn/
Mach schürtzbeltz /brustthůch/Vehehaubn/
Von Zöbel/Marder/Vehe vnd Lůchsen/
Von Hermlein/Jlter/Wölff vnd Füchsn/
Von Welschen Kröpffen vnd Geißfeln/
Von Wammen/Rücken / Klaw vnd Keln/
Wer mir thut seines Geltes gönnen/
Der thut mich allzeit willig finden.

THE FURRIER makes and lines coats, cloaks, hoods and other garments
with such furs as sable, marten, lynx, ermine, polecat, wolf and fox,
and from goatskins.

Der Schwartzferber.

Ich bin der schwartz Farb ein Sücher/
Ferb den Kauffleutn die Schwabnthücher
Grün/graw vnd schwartz/ vñ darzu blaw/
Darzu ich auch ein Mange hab/
Daß ich sie mang fein gell vnd glat/
Auch was man sonst zu ferben hat/
Vnd mangen findt man mich allzeit/
Darzu gutwillig vnd bereit.

N iij   Der

THE DYER dyes cloth various colors for merchants, and also presses and
smoothes cloth.

Der Weber.

Ich bin ein Weber zu Leinen Wat/
Kan wircken Barchent vnd Sponat/
Tischthücher/ Handzwehl/ Facilet/
Vnd wer luſt zu Bettziechen hett/
Gewürffelt oder Kamaca/
Allerley gmödelt Thücher da/
Auch Flechſen vnd wircken Haußthuch/
Die Kunſt ich bey Aragnes ſuch.

Der

THE WEAVER makes linen clothing in fustian and other weaves, table-
cloths, towels and coverlets, in checks and other patterns; weaving
was invented by Aragnes [Arachne].

Der Hüter.

Kehrt hie hereyn jr Kauffleut all/
Schauwt /ob mein arbeit euch gefall/
Von guter Wolln/sauber/nicht biltzet/
Wol gschlagen/gwalcken vnd gefiltzet/
Auch wol geformbt vnd zugericht/
Gezogen Hüt vnd auch gebicht/
Auch mach ich der Filtzsocken viel/
Wenn der kalt Winter anbrechn wil.

O   Der

THE HATTER makes well-shaped hats and warm socks of good wool felt.

Der Schuhmacher.

Hereyn/wer Stiffl vnd Schuh bedarff/
Die kan ich machen gut vnd scharff/
Büchsn / Armbrosthalffter vñ Wahtseck/
Feuwr Eymer vnd Reyßtruhen Deck/
Gewachtelt Reitstieffl / Kürißschuch/
Pantoffel / gefütert mit Thuch/
Wasserstiffl vnd Schuch außgeschnittn/
Frauwenschuch / nach Höflichen sittn.

D ij   Der

THE SHOEMAKER produces not only shoes, boots and slippers for all needs, but also such leather goods as bags, cases, crossbow holders and fire buckets.

Der Balbierer.

Ich bin beruffen allenthalbn/
Kan machen viel heilsamer Salbn/
Frisch wunden zu heiln mit Gnaden/
Dergleich Beinbrüch vnd alte Schaden/
Frantzosen heyln/den Staren stechn/
Den Brandt leschen vnd Zeen außbrechn/
Dergleich Balbiern/Zwagen vnd Schern
Auch Aderlassen thu ich gern.

                              O iij   Der

THE BARBER-SURGEON makes salves for wounds and broken limbs,
cures syphilis, operates for cataract, pulls teeth, cuts hair and bleeds
patients.

59

Der Zanbrecher.

Wolher/wer hat ein bösen Zan/
Denselben ich außbrechen kan/
On wehtagn / wie man gbiert die Kinder/
Auch hab ich Kramschatz nicht destminder/
Petrolium vnd Wurmsamen/
Thriacks vnd viel Mückenschwammen/
Hab auch gut Salbn / für Flöhe vñ Leuß/
Auch Puluer für Ratzen vnd Meuß.

Der

THE DENTIST removes aching teeth painlessly "as one bears children";
he also sells oils, salves and other medications, flea and louse ointments
and rat poison.

Der Bader.

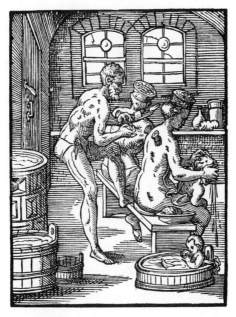

Wolher ins Bad Reich vnde Arm/
Das ist jetzund geheitzet warm/
Mit wolschmacker Laug mã euch wescht/
Denn auff die Oberbanck euch setzt/
Erschwitzt / deñ werdt jr zwagn vnd gribn/
Mit Lassn das vbrig Blut außtriebn/
Denn mit dem Wannenbad erfreuwt/ -
Darnach geschorn vnd abgeflehe.

P   Der

THE BATHHOUSE PROPRIETOR washes rich and poor alike in his well-heated establishment, gives them sweatbaths and rubdowns, bleeds them, cuts their hair and rids them of fleas.

61

Der Glockengiesser.

Ich kan mancherley Glocken gießn/
Auch Büchsen/darauß man thut schießn/
Auch Mörser/damit man würfft Feuwr
Zu den Feinden / gar vngeheuwr/
Auch Ehrn Häfen auff dreyen beyn/
Auch Ehrin öfen / groß vnd klein/
Auß Glocken Ertz/künstlich gegoßn/
Lydus hat diese Kunst außgoßn.

P ij　　　　Der

THE BELL FOUNDER makes bells, rifles, mortars, cauldrons and ovens of
all sizes out of bell metal; this art was invented by Lydus.

Der Fingerhüter

Auß Messing mach ich Fingerhüt/
Blechweiß / werden im Feuwer glüt/
Denn in das Eysen glenck getriebn/
Darnach löchlein darein gehiebn/
Gar mancherly art / eng vnd weit/
Für Schuster vnd Schneider bereit/
Für Seidensticker vnd Näterin/
Deß Handwercks ich ein Meister bin.

Der

THE THIMBLE MAKER manufactures his products from brass which is
heated, shaped and riddled with holes; they are used by cobblers, tailors,
embroiderers and seamstresses.

Der Läderer.

Die Heuwt die henck ich in den Bach/
Werff sie in den Escher darnach /
Dergleich die Kalbfel auch also/
Darnach wirff ich sie in das Loh/
Da sie jr ruhe ein zeit erlangn/
Darnach henck ichs auff an die Stangn/
Wüsch darnach ab mit eim Harwüsch/
Vnd habs feyl auff dem Leder Tisch.

Der

THE TANNER soaks the hides in a stream, throws them into the lime,
leaves them a long time in the tan, then dries them on poles.

Der Brillenmacher.

Ich mach gut Brillen / klar vnd liecht/
Auff mancherley Alter gericht/
Von viertzig biß auff achtzig jarn/
Darmit das gsicht ist zu bewarn/
Die gheuß von Leder oder Horn/
Dreyn die gläser Poliert sind worn/
Dadurch man sicht/gar hell vnd scharff/
Die find ihr hie / wer der bedarff.
            Q   Der

THE SPECTACLES MAKER makes eyeglasses of different strengths for people from forty to eighty; the frames are of leather or horn.

Der Bürstenbinder.

Ein Bürstenbinder nennt man mich/
Allerley gattung mache ich/
Schön bürsten für Frauwn vn jůckfrauwn
Mit Golt vmbzogn lustig zuschauwn/
Auch Kehrbürstn für die Kleider lind/
Auch Börstwůsch für das Haußgesind/
Auch Bürstn damit mã Gläser schwencke
Wo die mit vnlust wern behenckt.

Q ij   Der

THE BRUSH MAKER manufactures brushes of all qualities for all purposes, from gold-mounted hairbrushes to brushes for scouring glasses.

Der Kammacher.

Kam machen hab gelehrnet ich/
Buchßbäumen Kem/ gar Meisterlich/
Auch Hürnen Kem für die Gemein/
Auch schöne Kem von Helffenbeyn/
Für Balbierer vnd grosse Herrn/
Die schön ding haben wunder gern/
Also mancher gattung zumal/
Find jr auch bey mir ohne zal.

Q iij   Der

THE COMB MAKER manufactures combs of boxwood, of horn for commoners, of ivory for barbers and wealthy families, and many other kinds.

Der Thuchschärer.

Hereyn/wer Thuch zu schären hab/
Es sey Schwartz/Grün/Rot oder Blaw/
Mechlisch/ Lündisch/ Lyrisch / Stamet/
Englisch / vnd wie es namen het/
Auch Barchant schmitzn vnd kutniren/
Kan schmaltzfleck außreyben vñ schmiern/
Die Hosenfell auch Künstlich schmitzn/
Vnd Kittelthuch/daß es thut glitzn.

Der

THE CLOTH SHEARER shears cloth of all weaves and colors for his customers, pleats material and also removes stains from cloth.

Der Schloffer.

Ich mach die Schlothüt klein vnd groß/
Rigel/Bender/Schlüssel vnd Schloß/
Eysern Truhen/Bruñketin/Gitter/
Scheid auch die Schlöt/ für vngwitter/
Kuchentryfus/Eysern Bräter/
Den Kirchen Han/zeygt Wind vñ wettr/
Auch Ofenfüß/ was man wil han/
Von Eysen ich wol machen kan.

R   Der

THE LOCKSMITH makes locks, keys, bolts, chains, iron chests, grates,
weathercocks and many other iron objects.

Der Circkelschmidt.

Ich mach mancherley Werckzeug art/
Subtile Zirckel vnd Daßart/
Mancherley Zangen / gschraufft vñ glatt/
Dreh Eyßn/Gärb Eyßn/in vil Werckstat/
Dem holtzdrechßl/rotschmidt vñ schreiner/
Kandelgiesser vnd Balbierer/
Mach auch künstlicher Stück sehr viel/
Rein gegraben/glatt vnd subtil.

R ij   Der

THE TOOLMAKER manufactures compasses, tongs, pliers and other
tools for turners, joiners, pewterers, barbers and other artisans.

Der Messerschmidt.

Ich mach Par messer wol beschalt/
Köstlich vnd schlecht / darnach mans zalt/
Von Helffenbeyn/ Buchßbaü vñ Sandl/
Mit rot vnd schwartzem Holtz ohn wandl/
Mach darzu Langwehr / Dolch vñ Tegn/
Kan etȝ/ Scheyd machn/ vñ Schwert segȇ
Wer dieser meiner arbeit darff/
Der find mein Zeichen grecht vnd scharff.
K iij   Der

THE CUTLER makes knives with handles of ivory, boxwood, sandalwood
and other woods; he also makes spears, daggers, swords and scabbards,
and etches and cleans swords.

Der Sporer.

Ich mache Sporn von Stahl vñ Eyßn/
Geschwertzt vñ Zint/die man thut preyßn/
Die doch den Gaul nit hart verletzn/
Welch Pferd sich tückisch widersetzn/
Den mach ich ein scharffes gebiß/
Das jn von statten treibt gewiß:
Dem Bauwren mach ichs gröber viel/
Der es nur wolfeyl haben wil.

Der

THE SPUR MAKER manufactures steel and iron spurs and bits—cheaper
ones for farmers.

Der Kupfferschmidt.

Ich mach auff hohe Thürn die Knöpff/
Eymer damit man Brünnen schöpfft/
Badkeßll / Trög vnd die Badwannen/
Feuwr Kuffen / Breuwkeßl Pfannen/
Klein vnd groß Kessel zu dem waschen/
Hellhäffn / Kůlkeßl/ vnd Weinflaschen/
Fleischscheffel / Spůlnepff/ waßer Stůtz/
Brennhůt zum Waßer brennen nütz.

                            S   Der

THE COPPERSMITH makes pails, basins, troughs, bathtubs, vats, pans, washtubs, wine bottles, stills and many other products.

Der Büchsenschmidt.

Ich bin aber ein Büchsen Schmid/
Die Büchsen Ror die mach ich mit/
Kurtz vnd lang/ Eysern/ starck vnd fest/
Außbort/ auff das gletteft vnd best/
Der keines ist mir feil darbey/
Biß es vor wol beschossen sey/
Auff daß im schuß es nit zerspring/
Vnd einen Mann zu schaden bring.

S ij   Der

THE GUNSMITH makes excellent guns which he tests before selling to
prevent injury to the purchaser.

Der Vhrmacher.

Jch mache die reysenden Vhr/
Gerecht vnd Glatt nach der Mensur/
Von hellem glaß vnd kleim Vhrsant/
Gut/daß sie haben langen bestandt/
Mach auch darzu Hültzen Geheuß/
Dareyn ich sie fleissig beschleuß/
Ferb die gheuß Grün/Graw/rot vñ blaw
Drinn man die Stund vnd vierteil hab.

S iij   Der

THE CLOCKMAKER manufactures hourglasses, and builds and paints
wooden cases for his carefully made timepieces.

Der Rotschmidt.

Bildwerck/Wappen/ich goſſen hab/
Auff mannig köſtlich Fürſten Grab/
Artlich Leuchter / ſo ſtehn vnd hangn/
In Kirchen vnd auff dem Sal brangn/
Räuchfeſſer vnd die Meſſing Sprützn/
Die man thut in den Brünſten nützen/
Mörſer/ Leimtigl vnd Schüſſel Ring/
Pippen/ Laßköff/ vnd ander ding.

Der

THE METALWORKER makes statuettes, coats-of-arms for noblemen's tombs, candlesticks, censers, firehose nozzles, keyrings and many other objects.

Der Nagler.

Ein Nagelſchmid bin ich genannt/
Mach eyſern Negel mit der Hand/
Allerley art auff meim Amboß/
Kurtz vnde Lang/Klein vnd auch Groß
Bůhnnegel / Schloßnegel/ darzu
Faßnegl / Schuchzweck/ich machen thu/
Halbnegel / pfeningnegel ſtarck/
Find man bey mir / an offnem Marck.

T Der

THE NAIL MAKER produces all sizes of nails and tacks for builders, coopers, shoemakers and other artisans.

Der Sensenschmidt.

Vil Sensen durch mich gschmidet sind/
Mit Hämerschlagen/ schnell vñ schwind/
Die Dengel ich scharff vber dmaß/
Damit man Mecht das grüne Graß/
Darauß denn wirt Grumaht vnd Heuw/
Auch mach ich Sichel mancherley/
Darmit man einschneid das Getreid/
Durch alte Weiber vnd Bauwrn Meid.

Der

THE SCYTHE MAKER manufactures well-sharpened scythes and sickles
for mowing and harvesting.

Der Blatner.

Gut Stehle Harnisch ich schlagē kan/
Beyde für Roß vnd auch für Mann/
Gantze Küriß vnd die Roßpar/
In die Schlacht/wol versorget gar/
Auch zun Thurnir / Stechn vnd Rennen/
Sonst allr art / wie mans mag nennen/
Für den Gmein hauffen/schlecht gemacht/
Das habn die Spartaner auff bracht.

T iij   Der

THE ARMORER makes steel armor for men and horses for use in war
or tourneys (cheaper items for commoners): this art was invented by
the Spartans.

Der Schmidt.

Ich Huff schmidt kä die pferd beschlagn/
Darzu die Räder / Karn vnd Wagn/
Schwäntzen vnd Lassen ich wol kan/
Den Pferden / die auch Schäden han/
Ich kan heyln / Retzen vnd Reiden/
Den Feyfel vnd die Angstel schneidn/
Zu den Ciclopen trag ich Gunst/
Die erfunden deß Schmidwercks Kunst.

Der

THE BLACKSMITH makes horseshoes and wagon wheels, clips horses' tails and treats ailing horses; smithing was invented by the Cyclopes.

Der Beckſchlager.

Ein Beckſchlager bin ich genannt/
Mein Beckn führt man in weite Land/
Allerley art / groß vnd auch klein/
Von gutem Meſſing gſchlagen rein/
Geſtempfft mit bildwerck/gwechß vñ blũ/
Einstheils ir Spigel glatt auff kum/
Wie groß Herrn vnd Balbierer han/
Auch gring / für den gemeinen Mann.

V   Der

THE BASIN MAKER decorates his brass wares, which are exported far
and wide, with stamped foliage and flowers; they are of different quality
depending on the income of the purchaser.

Der Schellenmacher.

Ich aber bin ein Schellenmachr/
Zu Preng vnd Narrnweiß ein vrsachr/
Mach Zimbel Schellen/groß vnd klein/
Zum Schlittenzeug / sauber vnd rein/
Auch wol gestimbt auff die Stech Bahn/
Darzu Schelln für den Prittschenmann/
Auch Schellen an die Narren Kappn/
Darmits zu Faßnacht vmbher sappn.

V ij   Der

THE BELL MAKER makes small bells for tambourines, sleighs, tourneys, harlequins and Carnival fools' caps.

Der Kandelgiesser.

Das Zin mach ich im Feuwer fließn/
Thu darnach in die Mödel gießn/
Kandel/Flaschen/groß vnd auch klein/
Darauß zu trincken Bier vnd Wein/
Schüssel/Blatten/Täller/der maß/
Schenck Kandel/Saltzfaß vnd Gießfaß/
Ohlbüchßn/Leuchter vnd Schüsselring/
Vnd sonst ins Hauß fast nütze ding.

B iij   Der

THE PEWTERER melts the pewter, then pours it into molds for flagons and bottles, keys, keyrings, platters, pitchers, salt cellars, candlesticks and other useful items for the home.

Der Nadler.

Ich mach Nadel auß Eysendrat
Schneid die leng jeder gattung glatt/
Darnach ichs feyl / mach ôhr vnd spitzn/
Alßdann hert ichs ins Feuwers hitzn/
Darnach sind sie feil / zu verkauffn/
Die Krämer holen sie mit hauffn/
Auch grobe Nadel neñen hin/
Die Ballenbinder vnd Beuwrin.

Der

THE NEEDLE MAKER cuts the needles from iron wire, files them, makes
eyes and sharpens the points, then strengthens them by heating; they
are purchased in quantity by peddlers.

Der Pantzermacher.

Ich bin ein Pantzermacher frembd/
Ich mach die Stählen Pantzerhembd/
Auch Pantzer Ermel vnd Pantzerstrich/
Die man tregt/offen vnd heimlich/
Auch von Pantzer gut Stählen Krägn/
Ich kan auch Pantzer rolln vnd fegn/
Wo sie mit Rost anlauffen thon/
Midias Pantzermachn fieng an.

X   Der

THE ARMOR WORKER makes shirts, armpieces and collars for suits of armor; he also removes rust from armor; Midias invented this art.

Der Pogner.

Gut Armbroſter kan machen ich/
Die Seulen zier ich fleiſſiglich/
Mit gwechs/ſchneweiſſem bein durchzogn/
Mit Hürnen oder Sthälen pogn/
Darauff windfadn vnd ein Sännen/
Die nicht leichtlich iſt zutrennen/
Darmit man gwiß zum Ziel mag ſchießn/
Der Kunſt Syrus wir mit genießn.

X ij   Der

THE CROSSBOW MAKER uses very tough strings and bows of horn or
steel; his art was invented by Syrus.

Der Wägleinmacher.

Ich mach die Wag / groß vnde klein/
Mit allerley Gwicht in gemein/
Die behenck ich mit Messingschaln/
Wo man mirs anderß thut bezaln/
Mach auch in die Lädlein Goltwag/
Nach den haben die Kauffleut frag/
Darzu ander Würtzwäglein gut/
Die man in Krämen brauchen thut.
                    X iij   Der

THE SCALE MAKER produces many different kinds of balances for many
uses, including merchants' scales for weighing gold and grocers' scales
for spices.

Der Laternmacher.

Ich mach die groß künstlich Latern/
In Kirchen leuchtend klar Lucern/
Mach auch die blind Latern / gestaucht/
Die man in dem FeltLäger braucht/
Schön Liechtkolben ich auch bereit/
Bey Nacht / zu Gastung vnd Hochzeit/
Darzu Latern groß vnde klein/
So man zu Nacht braucht / in Gemein.

Der

THE LANTERN MAKER manufactures everyday lanterns, large artistic
church lanterns, dark lanterns for military use and fancy lights for
festivities.

Der Sattler.

Wolher/wer Sättel hab zumachn/
Den Edlen/vnd zu Reysing sachn/
Schön Sättl für das Frauwenzimmer/
Darauff sie Höflich prangn jmmer/
Auch Stächsättel/ vnd zum Thurnier/
Allerley art findt jr bey mir/
Auch Sättel für Bauwrn vnd Fuhrleut/
Gut Roß Kumaht ich auch anbeut.

Y   Der

THE SADDLER makes fine saddles for ladies, special jousting saddles,
saddles for farmers and carters.

Der Hafner.

Den Leymen tritt ich mit meim Fuß
Mit Har gemischt/ darnach ich muß
Ein klumpen werffen auff die Scheiben
Die muß ich mit den Füssen treiben/
Mach Krüg/ Häffen/ Kachel vñ Scherbē
Thu sie denn glassurn vnd ferben/
Darnach brenn ich sie in dem Feuwer/
Corebus gab die Kunst zu steuwer.

                    Y ij   Der

THE POTTER treads the clay (mixed with hair) and puts it on his wheel, which he drives with his foot; the shaped pieces (jars, pots, tiles) are glazed, painted and fired; the art was invented by Corebus.

Der Spiegler.

Ich mach das helle Spiegelglaß/
Mit Bley ichs vnderziehen laß/
Vnd drehe darnach die Hültzen Scheibn/
Darinn die Spiegelgläßer bleibn/
Die Mal ich denn mit Farben frey/
Feuwer Spiegel mach ich darbey/
Darinn das Angsicht groß erschein/
Daß mans sicht eigentlich vnd fein.

                              Y iij   Der

THE MIRROR MAKER builds and paints the frames as well as making the
reflecting glasses, including magnifying mirrors.

Der Schleyffer.

Ich schleiff sehr scharff auff mein schleyff
Messerklingē/mittl/groß vnd klein/ stein
Feyln/Schlösser/bender allewegn/
Helleparten/Dolch / Schwert vnd Degn/
Allen Harnisch zu Fuß vnd Roß/
Halb vnd gantz Hacken/ zum geschoß
Reit Hämer/Partisan/ich zier/
Auch auff der Scheiben ich palier.

Der

THE GRINDER sharpens knives, files, halberds, daggers, swords, parts
of armor and so on.

Der Steynmetz.

Ich bin ein Steynmetz lange zeit/
Mit stangn/Winckelmäß vñ Richtscheit/
Ich auffricht Steinheuser wolbsinn/
Mit Keller/gewelb/Bad vnd Brünn/
Mit Gibelmauwrn von Quaderstein/
Auch Schlösser vnd Thürnen ich meyn/
Setz ich auff festen starcken grundt/
Cadmus erstlich die Kunst erfund.

Z   Der

THE STONEMASON, using builder's tools, erects stone houses, castles, towers, all on firm foundations; the art was invented by Cadmus.

Der Ziegler.

Ein Ziegler thut man mich nennen/
Auß Lättn kan ich Ziegel brennen/
Gelatt vnd hell/ Kälend darbey/
Daschen Ziegl/ auch sonst mancherley/
Damit man deckt die Heusser obn/
Für Regen/ Schnee vnd Windes thobn/
Auch für der heyssen Sonnen schein/
Cynira erfund die Kunst allein.

THE BRICKMAKER bakes smooth bricks and rooftiles from clay; the art
was invented by Cynira.

Der Zimmermann.

Ich Zimmermann / mach starck gebeuw/
In Schlösser/Heusser/alt vnd neuw/
Ich mach auch mancherley Mülwerck/
Auch Windmüln oben auff die Berg/
Vber die Wasser starcke Brückn/
Auch Schiff vnd Flöß/von freyen stückn/
Blochheusser zu der gegenwehr/
Dedalus gab mir diese Lehr.

Z iij

Der

THE CARPENTER builds houses, mills, bridges, ships, rafts, blockhouses;
Daedalus invented the art.

Der Schreiner.

Ich bin ein Schreinr von Nürenberg/
Von Flader mach ich schön Teflwerck/
Verschrottn/vnd versetzt mit zier/
Leisten vnd Sims auff Welsch monier/
Thruhen/Schubladn/Gwandbehalter/
Tisch/Bettstat/Brettspiel Gießkalter/
Gesirneust/ köstlich oder schlecht/
Eim jeden vmb sein pfenning recht.

Der

THE JOINER from Nuremberg makes fine varnished furniture with fancy
moldings: chests, wardrobes, dressers, tables, beds, board games, etc.,
for all purses.

Der Wagner.

Ich mach Räder/Wägen vnd Kärrn/
Roll vnd Reyßwägen / für groß Herrn/
Kammerwägen / den Frauwen klug/
Auch mach ich dem Bauwren den Pflug/
Vnd darzu auch Schleyfen vnd Egn/
Thus als mit gutem Holtz verlegn/
Ich arbeit hart bey meinen tagn/
Friges erfundn erstlich den Wagn.

         a   Der

THE WAGONWRIGHT makes wheels and all sorts of carriages, wagons
and carts, ploughs and harrows; the wagon was invented by Friges.

Der Bütner.

Ich bin ein Bütner / vnd mach stoltz/
Auß Förhen / Tennen / Eichen Holtz/
Badwañ/ Schmaltzkübl/ scheffel vñ gelten/
Die Bütten vnd Weinfässer / welten/
Bier Fässer machn / bichen vnd binden/
Waschzübr thut man bey mir finden/
Auch mach ich lägl / Fässer vnd Stübch/
Gen Franckfurt / Leipzig vnd Lübig.

THE COOPER uses Scotch pine, fir and oak to make barrels, tubs, beer
and wine casks, which are shipped to Frankfurt, Leipzig and Lübeck.

Der Holtzdrechßler.

Ich dreh von Buchßbaum büchßlein
Zu kleinot vnd Edlem gestein/   (klein
Auch Futteral/ zu Gülden Scheuwrn/
Predigstül/ dran man sich kan steuwrn/
Köstlich Stolln / zu Tisch vnd Betten/
Hämmerstiel / so die Goldschmid hettn/
Auch für die Bauwrn Kugel vnd Kegl/
Wellen/ vnd auch Steynmetz Schlegel.
a iij   Der

THE TURNER makes little jewel boxes of boxwood, cases, pulpits, bed-
posts, hammer handles, bowling pins, mallets.

Der Büchsenschäffter.

Die Eyfern Rohr kan ich eynfaßn/
In Hültzen Schäfft / künftlicher maßn/
Mit verschrottem werck / sauber rein/
Mit eingelegtem Helffenbein/
Kurtz vnde lang / klein vnde groß/
Die man führet zu Fuß vnd Roß/
Wohin reyset ein ehrlich Mann/
Sich der Räuber auff halten kan.

Der

THE RIFLE BUTT MAKER mounts the iron rifle barrels in artistically
finished butts with inlaid ivory; thus honest men can ward off robbers.

Der Permennter.

Ich kauff Schaffell/Böck/vñ die Geiß/
Die Fell leg ich denn in die beyß/
Darnach firm ich sie sauber rein/
Spann auff die Ram jeds Fell allein/
Schabs darnach/mach Permennt darauß/
Mit grosser arbeit in mein Hauß/
Auß ohrn vnd klauwen seud ich Leim/
Das alles verkauff ich daheim.

b   Der

THE PARCHMENT MAKER places sheep and goat skins in lime, washes
them, stretches them on the frame and scrapes them; the ears and
paws are boiled into glue.

Der Sieber.

Ich muß am tag viel Höltzer kliebn/
Zu dünnen Spänen zu den Siebn/
Vnd zu zargen oben herumb/
Der Sieb mach ich ein grosse Summ/
In die Mülen/ auch zu den Beckn/
Das Mehl zuscheyden in den seckn/
Mach auch Würtz Sieblein in die Krām/
Grob Rätten ich den Bauwren nem.

Der

THE SIEVE MAKER saws wood very thin for the sides of his sieves, which
are used for bolting flour in mills and sifting spices in grocers' shops;
he makes coarse sieves for farmers.

Der Seyler.

Ich bin ein Seyler / der zum theil/
Kan machen die langen Schiff Seyl/
Auch Seyl zum bauw / dran man allein
Auffziech Mörder /Zimerholtz vñ Stein/
Ich kan auch machen Garn vnd Netz/
Zur Jägerey vnd zu der Hetz/
Darzu auch Fisch Netz / groß vnd klein/
Sonst auch allerley Strick gemein.

Der

THE ROPEMAKER produces heavy ropes for ships and for hoisting construction materials, snares and nets for hunting and fishing and all sorts of ropes and cords.

103

Der Schiffmann.

Im Meer bin ich ein Schiff Patron/
In dem Compastich sehen kan
Wo wir im Meer jrr gfaren sind/
Wenn sich erhebet ein Sturmwind/
Mit grossen Welln vns wil bedeckn/
Den Ancker wir im Meer einsenckn/
Auff daß das Schiff vnbweglich steh/
Biß die grausam Fortun vergehe.

Der

THE SEA CAPTAIN guides his vessel by means of the compass and
casts anchor when there is a storm.

Der Fiſcher.

Ich fach gute Fiſch ohn mangel/
Mit der Setz/Reußen/vnd dem Angl/
Grundel/Sengel/Erlen vnd Kreſſn/
Forhen/Eſch/Ruppen/ Hecht vnd Preſſn/
Barben / Karpffen / thu ich behaltn/
Orphen/Neunaugen/Ehl vnd Altn/
Kugelhaupt/ Naſen/ Hauſn vnd Huchn,
Krebs mag man auch bey mir ſuchen.

c   Der

THE FISHERMAN uses rod, net and weir to catch a wide variety of species
including pike, carp, eels, lampreys and crabs.

Der Ölmacher.

Mancherley öl ich zubereit
Zu essen vnd zu Artzeney allzeit/
Als Baumöl / Nußöl vnd Pinöl
Loröl/ Hanfföl/ Leinöl / da soll
Ich die Beer samlen vnvergessen
Zermalmen / vnd darnach außpressen/
Darmit das öl ich darauß bring/
Minerua erfund diese ding.

THE OIL MAKER gathers, crushes and presses many kinds of fruits and seeds to produce edible and medicinal oils; the art was invented by Minerva.

Der Rebmann.

Ich bin ein Häcker im Weinberg
Im Früling hab ich harte werck/
Mit graben/ pältzen vnd mit hauwen/
Mit Pfälstossn/ pflantzen vnd bauwen/
Mit auffbinden vnd schneiden die Reben/
Biß im Herbst die Traubn Wein geben:
Den man schneidt vnd außprest deñ fein.
Noa erfand erstlich den Wein.

THE VINEGROWER must hack, dig, plant, prop, graft, bind and prune
in springtime in order to have wine in autumn; Noah first discovered
wine.

Die Singer.

Gut Gefang habn wir hie notirt/
Das in vier Stiñ gefungen wirdt/
Tenor/ Difcant / Alt vnd der Baß/
Mit fchön höfflichen Text dermaß/
So lieblich zufammen concordirt/
Vnd alfo vberfüß fonirt/
Daß fich ein Hertz erhebt dar von/
Das Gefang erfund Amphion.

Die

THE SINGERS are performing a four-part work (tenor, discant, alto, bass) with a fine courtly text; their harmony gives joy to the heart; Amphion invented song.

Dratzieher.

Den Drat/Kupffer vnd Messing rein/
Zeuch ich auff meiner Scheiben klein/
Mach Röllen Drat/Zin jn vnd Wid/
Vnd Dratbürsten für die Goldschmidt/
Auch kommn meiner quintsaiten suß
Herrlich auff das Claucordium/
Auß kleinem Drat man an viel orten
Macht Hutschnür vñ gedrungen Borten.
d   Der

THE WIREDRAWER produces copper and brass wire on his wheel; he
makes twisted wire and other types, wire brushes for goldsmiths, clavi-
chord strings; small wires are also used in hatmaking.

Der Hefftelmacher.

Ich mach Steckhefft auß Messing drat/
Fein außgebutzt/rund/sauber/glatt/
Mit runden Knöpfflein gut vnd scharpff/
Aller art wie man der bedarff/
Auch mach ich Hackn vnd schleifflein gut
Gschwertzt vnd geziert/darmit man thut
Sich eynbrüsten Weib vnd auch Mann/
Daß die Kleider glatt ligen an.

THE PINMAKER produces fine, smooth, round-headed pins out of brass
wire; he also makes clasps for clothing.

Der Lautenmacher.

Gut Lauten hab ich lang gemacht
Auß Tännenholtz/gut vnd geschlacht/
Erstlich vber die Form gebogn/
Darnach mit Saiten vberzogn/
Vnd angestimmt mit süssem Klang/
Eben gleich figuriertem Gsang/
Gefürnist Kragen/Bodn vnd Stern/
Auch mach ich Geigen vnd Quintern.

Der

THE LUTHIER makes lutes by bending fir wood over a block, putting on
the strings and varnishing; he also makes bowed string instruments
and guitars.

Der Bergknapp.

Ich treib alles Ertz Knappenwerck/
Im Thal vnd auff Sanct Annen Berg/
Mit den Steigern/Knappen vnd Bubn
In Stollen/Schacht vnd den Ertzgrubn/
Mit graben/zimmern/böltzn vnd bauwn/
Mit eynfahren/ brechen vnd hauwn/
Wird ich fündig vnd Silber bring/
So ist der Bergherr guter ding.

Der

THE MINER works in the valley and on the Sankt Annenberg, in tunnels,
shafts and quarries.

Der Organiſt.

Das Poſitiff mit ſüſſem hal/
Schlag ich auff Bürgerlichem Sal/
Da die ehrbarn der Gſchlecht ſind gſeſſn/
Ein köſtlich Hochzeitmal zu eſſen/
Daß jn die weil nicht werd zu lang
Brauchn wir die Leyern mit geſang/
Daß ſich darvon jr Hertz eben/
In freud vnd wunne thu erhebn.

e   Harpff

THE ORGANIST plays the positive at the wedding banquets of the gentry,
at which singers and string players also perform.

Harpffen vnd Lauten.

Wir schlagen nach der Tablatur/
Nach der Noten rechter Mensur/
Daß die Lauten vnd auch die Harpff
Geben jr Concordantz fein scharpff/
Mit gschwinden leufflein auff vnd nidr/
Nach deß Gsangs art hin vnd wider/
Singn wir Carmina mit dem Mund/
Orpheus die schöne kunst erfundt.

e   ij   Drey

HARP AND LUTE PLAYERS follow the written score in creating their
harmonious music, which includes rapid scale passages; they sometimes
vocalize; Orpheus invented the art.

Drey Geiger.

Die Geigen wir gar künstlich ziehn
Daß all schwermütigkeit muß fliehn/
Wie sie erklingen künstlich gantz
An einem Adelichen Tantz/
Mit leisen tritten höflichen prangen/
Hertzlieb sein Hertzlieb thut vmbfangen
Das Hertz vnd Gmüt sich freuwen muß/
Vnd tantzen mit geringem Fuß.

e iij   Pfeiffen

THREE STRING PLAYERS perform their courtly dance so well that melancholy flees and the dancing couples are overjoyed.

Drey Pfeiffer.

Mit gar lieblicher Melodey
So pfeiffen wir hie alle drey/
Mit Schwegel/Zincken vñ zwerchpfeiffen
Darmit wir gar gründtlich ergreiffn/
Die Thon der Lieder componirt/
Vnd der Lieb darmit wirt hofiert/
Der zarten Frauwen roter Mund/
Pan der Gott die Pfeiffen erfund.

                        Herdrum»

THREE WIND PLAYERS are performing on tabor, cornet *(Zink)* and transverse flute; Pan invented musical pipes.

Heertrummel.

Mein Heertrummel die laß ich brommen/
Bald der Adl auff die Bahn ist kommen/
Zu thurniren/rennen vnd stechen
In Schilt vñ Helm die Spär zubrechen/
Dergleich wo sie zu feld auch ligen/
Gegen dem feind in den Kriegen/
Mit der Heertrummel das hertz ich weck
Der vnsern/vnd die feind erschreck.

f   Der

THE KETTLEDRUMMER plays at jousts and tourneys and on campaigns
to hearten friends and dismay foes.

Der Teppichmacher.

Ich mach der Teppich mancherley/
Köftlich/ mittel / vnd rein darbey/
Auß wüllem Garn vber Bett vnd Tifch/
Von farben schön/tunckel vnd frisch/
Mit Bildung/ gwächß vñ schön blumen/
Die in Egypten seind auff kummn/
Vor vil jaren vnd langer zeit/
Der jetzt auch vil das Teutschland geit.

f ij   Der

THE TAPESTRY WEAVER makes woolen coverings with colors and patterns for beds and tables; this art originated in Egypt.

Der Geltnarr.

Ein Geltnarr so werd ich genannt/
On ruh ist mein hertz/mund vnd hand/
Wie ich nur groß Gelt vnd Reichthumb
Vnverschempt listig vberkumb/
Mit dem Jüdenspieß thu ich lauffn/
Mit Wucher/ auffsätzn vnd verkauffn/
Bin doch darbey sehr genauw vnd karck/
Ich spar das gut vnd friß das arg.

f iij   Der

THE MONEY FOOL things of nothing but the acquisition of money by means fair or foul; he practices usury and hoards his money, denying himself good things.

119

Der Freſſend Narr.

Ich bin genennt der Freſſend Narr/
Man kennt mich in der gantzen Pfarr/
Wo mich ein reich Mann lett zu tiſch/
Setzt mir für gut Wildpret vnd fiſch/
So ſchlem ich ſam wolt mirs entlauffn/
Thu auch den Wein ſo knollicht ſauffn/
Als ob ich ſey gantz bodenloß/
Deß iſt mein Schmerbauch dick vnd groß.

Der

THE GLUTTONOUS FOOL, when invited to dine by a rich man, wolfs
down the food as if it were going to run away and swills the wine as if
he were bottomless: hence his paunch.

Der Schalcksnarr.

Ich brauch mancherley Narren weiß/
Darmit ich verdien Tranck vnd Speiß/
Doch weiß ich durch ein zaun mein Mañ/
Mit meim faßwerck zu greiffen an.
Da ich mit mein närrischen Sachn/
Die Herrschafft kan fein frölich machn/
Mit heuchlerey die Leut ich blendt/
Drumm man mich ein Schalcksnarren neñt.

g   Der

THE JESTER does all sorts of foolish things to entertain his master and thus earn his living, but there is hypocrisy in his craft.

Der Stocknarr.

Ein natürlich Stocknarr ich bin/
Denn ich hab weder Witz noch Sinn/
Hab ein groben verstand/der massen/
Kan weder hengen noch nachlassen/
Ich fahr herauß mit wort vnd that
Tölpischer weiß/ folg keinem raht/
Verschon niemand/drumb man mich zelt/
Für ein groben Stocknarren helt.

Beschluß.

THE NATURAL FOOL has no sense, acts and speaks without thinking,
and cannot follow advice.

Beschluß.

Also sind hie gezeiget an
Vierzehen vnd hundert Person/
In Emptern/ Künstin vñ Handarbeit
Doch vnderschieden ferr vnd weit/
Zu eim fürbild / daß jederman
Auff sich selb sol gut achtung han/
Daß in seinem Befelch vnd Ampt
Auß vnfleiß gar nichts werd versaumpt:
Dergleich Künstner vnd Handwercksleut/
Sollen auch handlen gar vertreuwt/
Einer dem andern dienen sol
Mit seiner arbeit recht vnd wol/
Wie er begert in rechter treuw
Vnd hab vor allen Lastern scheuw/
Als eigen nutz/ vnd müssig gan/
Weil Gott ein scheuwen hat daran/
Der vns herreicht in dieser zeit
Sein Brot durch viel mühe vnd arbeit/
Es sey so ring es immer wöll
Vns doch daran benützen sol
Gott darumb sagen Lob vnd Ehr/
Weil vns sein Hand alle ernehr:
Wer aber führt ein bösen Handel
Vnnütz/ Gottloß/ diesen Wandel

Auff das er nur groß Reichthumb hab
Der ker vmb/ vnd laß darvon ab
So entgeht er vil vngemachs/
Hie vnd auch dort/ so spricht Hans Sachß.

E N D E.

Gedruckt zu Franckfurt am
Meyn/ bey Georg Raben/ in
verlegung Sigmund Fey=
erabents.

M. D. LXVIII.

CONCLUSION

And so, dear reader, you have seen
One hundred persons and fourteen
In jobs, professions, Church and State—
The differences between them great—
As models whereby every man
In office his affairs may scan,
That they may not neglected be
Through want of needful industry.
Artists and craftsmen too should deal
With good faith and with honest zeal;
Let each of them the other aid
With work well done and things well made,
And as he would be served, thus serve.
Away from vices you should swerve,
Like selfishness and idle sloth,
For God above abhors them both,
And He it is who gives the bread
Which by our toil we've merited;
However little is supplied,
We still should be quite satisfied.
To God give honor and give praise:
His hand sustains us all our days.
But if you follow paths of bane,
Unprofitable, godless, vain,
In order to amass more pelf,
Turn back, desist, and save yourself
From hardships, troubles and attacks
On earth and after—says Hans Sachs.

Translation of colophon (page 124):

Printed in Frankfurt am Main in the shop of **Georg Raben**
for the publisher Sigmund Feyerabend.

Index of Ranks
and Occupations

A CATALOGUE OF SELECTED DOVER BOOKS
IN ALL FIELDS OF INTEREST

A CATALOGUE OF SELECTED DOVER BOOKS
IN ALL FIELDS OF INTEREST

AMERICA'S OLD MASTERS, James T. Flexner. Four men emerged unexpectedly from provincial 18th century America to leadership in European art: Benjamin West, J. S. Copley, C. R. Peale, Gilbert Stuart. Brilliant coverage of lives and contributions. Revised, 1967 edition. 69 plates. 365pp. of text.
21806-6 Paperbound $3.00

FIRST FLOWERS OF OUR WILDERNESS: AMERICAN PAINTING, THE COLONIAL PERIOD, James T. Flexner. Painters, and regional painting traditions from earliest Colonial times up to the emergence of Copley, West and Peale Sr., Foster, Gustavus Hesselius, Feke, John Smibert and many anonymous painters in the primitive manner. Engaging presentation, with 162 illustrations. xxii + 368pp.
22180-6 Paperbound $3.50

THE LIGHT OF DISTANT SKIES: AMERICAN PAINTING, 1760-1835, James T. Flexner. The great generation of early American painters goes to Europe to learn and to teach: West, Copley, Gilbert Stuart and others. Allston, Trumbull, Morse; also contemporary American painters—primitives, derivatives, academics—who remained in America. 102 illustrations. xiii + 306pp.
22179-2 Paperbound $3.00

A HISTORY OF THE RISE AND PROGRESS OF THE ARTS OF DESIGN IN THE UNITED STATES, William Dunlap. Much the richest mine of information on early American painters, sculptors, architects, engravers, miniaturists, etc. The only source of information for scores of artists, the major primary source for many others. Unabridged reprint of rare original 1834 edition, with new introduction by James T. Flexner, and 394 new illustrations. Edited by Rita Weiss. 6⅝ x 9⅝.
21695-0, 21696-9, 21697-7 Three volumes, Paperbound $13.50

EPOCHS OF CHINESE AND JAPANESE ART, Ernest F. Fenollosa. From primitive Chinese art to the 20th century, thorough history, explanation of every important art period and form, including Japanese woodcuts; main stress on China and Japan, but Tibet, Korea also included. Still unexcelled for its detailed, rich coverage of cultural background, aesthetic elements, diffusion studies, particularly of the historical period. 2nd, 1913 edition. 242 illustrations. lii + 439pp. of text.
20364-6, 20365-4 Two volumes, Paperbound $6.00

THE GENTLE ART OF MAKING ENEMIES, James A. M. Whistler. Greatest wit of his day deflates Oscar Wilde, Ruskin, Swinburne; strikes back at inane critics, exhibitions, art journalism; aesthetics of impressionist revolution in most striking form. Highly readable classic by great painter. Reproduction of edition designed by Whistler. Introduction by Alfred Werner. xxxvi + 334pp.
21875-9 Paperbound $2.50

VISUAL ILLUSIONS: THEIR CAUSES, CHARACTERISTICS, AND APPLICATIONS, Matthew Luckiesh. Thorough description and discussion of optical illusion, geometric and perspective, particularly; size and shape distortions, illusions of color, of motion; natural illusions; use of illusion in art and magic, industry, etc. Most useful today with op art, also for classical art. Scores of effects illustrated. Introduction by William H. Ittleson. 100 illustrations. xxi + 252pp.

21530-X Paperbound $2.00

A HANDBOOK OF ANATOMY FOR ART STUDENTS, Arthur Thomson. Thorough, virtually exhaustive coverage of skeletal structure, musculature, etc. Full text, supplemented by anatomical diagrams and drawings and by photographs of undraped figures. Unique in its comparison of male and female forms, pointing out differences of contour, texture, form. 211 figures, 40 drawings, 86 photographs. xx + 459pp. 5⅜ x 8⅜.

21163-0 Paperbound $3.50

150 MASTERPIECES OF DRAWING, Selected by Anthony Toney. Full page reproductions of drawings from the early 16th to the end of the 18th century, all beautifully reproduced: Rembrandt, Michelangelo, Dürer, Fragonard, Urs, Graf, Wouwerman, many others. First-rate browsing book, model book for artists. xviii + 150pp. 8⅜ x 11¼.

21032-4 Paperbound' $2.50

THE LATER WORK OF AUBREY BEARDSLEY, Aubrey Beardsley. Exotic, erotic, ironic masterpieces in full maturity: Comedy Ballet, Venus and Tannhauser, Pierrot, Lysistrata, Rape of the Lock, Savoy material, Ali Baba, Volpone, etc. This material revolutionized the art world, and is still powerful, fresh, brilliant. With *The Early Work*, all Beardsley's finest work. 174 plates, 2 in color. xiv + 176pp. 8⅛ x 11.

21817-1 Paperbound $3.00

DRAWINGS OF REMBRANDT, Rembrandt van Rijn. Complete reproduction of fabulously rare edition by Lippmann and Hofstede de Groot, completely reedited, updated, improved by Prof. Seymour Slive, Fogg Museum. Portraits, Biblical sketches, landscapes, Oriental types, nudes, episodes from classical mythology—All Rembrandt's fertile genius. Also selection of drawings by his pupils and followers. "Stunning volumes," *Saturday Review*. 550 illustrations. lxxviii + 552pp. 9⅛ x 12¼.

21485-0, 21486-9 Two volumes, Paperbound $10.00

THE DISASTERS OF WAR, Francisco Goya. One of the masterpieces of Western civilization—83 etchings that record Goya's shattering, bitter reaction to the Napoleonic war that swept through Spain after the insurrection of 1808 and to war in general. Reprint of the first edition, with three additional plates from Boston's Museum of Fine Arts. All plates facsimile size. Introduction by Philip Hofer, Fogg Museum. v + 97pp. 9⅜ x 8¼.

21872-4 Paperbound $2.00

GRAPHIC WORKS OF ODILON REDON. Largest collection of Redon's graphic works ever assembled: 172 lithographs, 28 etchings and engravings, 9 drawings. These include some of his most famous works. All the plates from *Odilon Redon: oeuvre graphique complet*, plus additional plates. New introduction and caption translations by Alfred Werner. 209 illustrations. xxvii + 209pp. 9⅛ x 12¼.

21966-8 Paperbound $4.00

DESIGN BY ACCIDENT; A BOOK OF "ACCIDENTAL EFFECTS" FOR ARTISTS AND DESIGNERS, James F. O'Brien. Create your own unique, striking, imaginative effects by "controlled accident" interaction of materials: paints and lacquers, oil and water based paints, splatter, crackling materials, shatter, similar items. Everything you do will be different; first book on this limitless art, so useful to both fine artist and commercial artist. Full instructions. 192 plates showing "accidents," 8 in color. viii + 215pp. 8⅜ x 11¼.   21942-9 Paperbound $3.50

THE BOOK OF SIGNS, Rudolf Koch. Famed German type designer draws 493 beautiful symbols: religious, mystical, alchemical, imperial, property marks, runes, etc. Remarkable fusion of traditional and modern. Good for suggestions of timelessness, smartness, modernity. Text. vi + 104pp. 6⅛ x 9¼.
                    20162-7 Paperbound $1.25

HISTORY OF INDIAN AND INDONESIAN ART, Ananda K. Coomaraswamy. An unabridged republication of one of the finest books by a great scholar in Eastern art. Rich in descriptive material, history, social backgrounds; Sunga reliefs, Rajput paintings, Gupta temples, Burmese frescoes, textiles, jewelry, sculpture, etc. 400 photos. viii + 423pp. 6⅜ x 9¾.   21436-2 Paperbound $4.00

PRIMITIVE ART, Franz Boas. America's foremost anthropologist surveys textiles, ceramics, woodcarving, basketry, metalwork, etc.; patterns, technology, creation of symbols, style origins. All areas of world, but very full on Northwest Coast Indians. More than 350 illustrations of baskets, boxes, totem poles, weapons, etc. 378 pp.
                    20025-6 Paperbound $3.00

THE GENTLEMAN AND CABINET MAKER'S DIRECTOR, Thomas Chippendale. Full reprint (third edition, 1762) of most influential furniture book of all time, by master cabinetmaker. 200 plates, illustrating chairs, sofas, mirrors, tables, cabinets, plus 24 photographs of surviving pieces. Biographical introduction by N. Bienenstock. vi + 249pp. 9⅞ x 12¾.   21601-2 Paperbound $4.00

AMERICAN ANTIQUE FURNITURE, Edgar G. Miller, Jr. The basic coverage of all American furniture before 1840. Individual chapters cover type of furniture— clocks, tables, sideboards, etc.—chronologically, with inexhaustible wealth of data. More than 2100 photographs, all identified, commented on. Essential to all early American collectors. Introduction by H. E. Keyes. vi + 1106pp. 7⅞ x 10¾.
                    21599-7, 21600-4 Two volumes, Paperbound $11.00

PENNSYLVANIA DUTCH AMERICAN FOLK ART, Henry J. Kauffman. 279 photos, 28 drawings of tulipware, Fraktur script, painted tinware, toys, flowered furniture, quilts, samplers, hex signs, house interiors, etc. Full descriptive text. Excellent for tourist, rewarding for designer, collector. Map. 146pp. 7⅞ x 10¾.
                    21205-X Paperbound $2.50

EARLY NEW ENGLAND GRAVESTONE RUBBINGS, Edmund V. Gillon, Jr. 43 photographs, 226 carefully reproduced rubbings show heavily symbolic, sometimes macabre early gravestones, up to early 19th century. Remarkable early American primitive art, occasionally strikingly beautiful; always powerful. Text. xxvi + 207pp. 8⅜ x 11¼.   21380-3 Paperbound $3.50

ALPHABETS AND ORNAMENTS, Ernst Lehner. Well-known pictorial source for decorative alphabets, script examples, cartouches, frames, decorative title pages, calligraphic initials, borders, similar material. 14th to 19th century, mostly European. Useful in almost any graphic arts designing, varied styles. 750 illustrations. 256pp. 7 x 10.   21905-4 Paperbound $4.00

PAINTING: A CREATIVE APPROACH, Norman Colquhoun. For the beginner simple guide provides an instructive approach to painting: major stumbling blocks for beginner; overcoming them, technical points; paints and pigments; oil painting; watercolor and other media and color. New section on "plastic" paints. Glossary. Formerly *Paint Your Own Pictures.* 221pp.   22000-1 Paperbound $1.75

THE ENJOYMENT AND USE OF COLOR, Walter Sargent. Explanation of the relations between colors themselves and between colors in nature and art, including hundreds of little-known facts about color values, intensities, effects of high and low illumination, complementary colors. Many practical hints for painters, references to great masters. 7 color plates, 29 illustrations. x + 274pp.
20944-X Paperbound $2.75

THE NOTEBOOKS OF LEONARDO DA VINCI, compiled and edited by Jean Paul Richter. 1566 extracts from original manuscripts reveal the full range of Leonardo's versatile genius: all his writings on painting, sculpture, architecture, anatomy, astronomy, geography, topography, physiology, mining, music, etc., in both Italian and English, with 186 plates of manuscript pages and more than 500 additional drawings. Includes studies for the Last Supper, the lost Sforza monument, and other works. Total of xlvii + 866pp. 7⅞ x 10¾.
22572-0, 22573-9 Two volumes, Paperbound $10.00

MONTGOMERY WARD CATALOGUE OF 1895. Tea gowns, yards of flannel and pillow-case lace, stereoscopes, books of gospel hymns, the New Improved Singer Sewing Machine, side saddles, milk skimmers, straight-edged razors, high-button shoes, spittoons, and on and on . . . listing some 25,000 items, practically all illustrated. Essential to the shoppers of the 1890's, it is our truest record of the spirit of the period. Unaltered reprint of Issue No. 57, Spring and Summer 1895. Introduction by Boris Emmet. Innumerable illustrations. xiii + 624pp. 8½ x 11⅝.
22377-9 Paperbound $6.95

THE CRYSTAL PALACE EXHIBITION ILLUSTRATED CATALOGUE (LONDON, 1851). One of the wonders of the modern world—the Crystal Palace Exhibition in which all the nations of the civilized world exhibited their achievements in the arts and sciences—presented in an equally important illustrated catalogue. More than 1700 items pictured with accompanying text—ceramics, textiles, cast-iron work, carpets, pianos, sleds, razors, wall-papers, billiard tables, beehives, silverware and hundreds of other artifacts—represent the focal point of Victorian culture in the Western World. Probably the largest collection of Victorian decorative art ever assembled— indispensable for antiquarians and designers. Unabridged republication of the Art-Journal Catalogue of the Great Exhibition of 1851, with all terminal essays. New introduction by John Gloag, F.S.A. xxxiv + 426pp. 9 x 12.
22503-8 Paperbound $4.50

A HISTORY OF COSTUME, Carl Köhler. Definitive history, based on surviving pieces of clothing primarily, and paintings, statues, etc. secondarily. Highly readable text, supplemented by 594 illustrations of costumes of the ancient Mediterranean peoples, Greece and Rome, the Teutonic prehistoric period; costumes of the Middle Ages, Renaissance, Baroque, 18th and 19th centuries. Clear, measured patterns are provided for many clothing articles. Approach is practical throughout. Enlarged by Emma von Sichart. 464pp.   21030-8 Paperbound $3.50

ORIENTAL RUGS, ANTIQUE AND MODERN, Walter A. Hawley. A complete and authoritative treatise on the Oriental rug—where they are made, by whom and how, designs and symbols, characteristics in detail of the six major groups, how to distinguish them and how to buy them. Detailed technical data is provided on periods, weaves, warps, wefts, textures, sides, ends and knots, although no technical background is required for an understanding. 11 color plates, 80 halftones, 4 maps. vi + 320pp. 6⅛ x 9⅛.   22366-3 Paperbound $5.00

TEN BOOKS ON ARCHITECTURE, Vitruvius. By any standards the most important book on architecture ever written. Early Roman discussion of aesthetics of building, construction methods, orders, sites, and every other aspect of architecture has inspired, instructed architecture for about 2,000 years. Stands behind Palladio, Michelangelo, Bramante, Wren, countless others. Definitive Morris H. Morgan translation. 68 illustrations. xii + 331pp.   20645-9 Paperbound $3.50

THE FOUR BOOKS OF ARCHITECTURE, Andrea Palladio. Translated into every major Western European language in the two centuries following its publication in 1570, this has been one of the most influential books in the history of architecture. Complete reprint of the 1738 Isaac Ware edition. New introduction by Adolf Placzek, Columbia Univ. 216 plates. xxii + 110pp. of text. 9½ x 12¾.
21308-0 Clothbound $10.00

STICKS AND STONES: A STUDY OF AMERICAN ARCHITECTURE AND CIVILIZATION, Lewis Mumford.One of the great classics of American cultural history. American architecture from the medieval-inspired earliest forms to the early 20th century; evolution of structure and style, and reciprocal influences on environment. 21 photographic illustrations. 238pp.   20202-X Paperbound $2.00

THE AMERICAN BUILDER'S COMPANION, Asher Benjamin. The most widely used early 19th century architectural style and source book, for colonial up into Greek Revival periods. Extensive development of geometry of carpentering, construction of sashes, frames, doors, stairs; plans and elevations of domestic and other buildings. Hundreds of thousands of houses were built according to this book, now invaluable to historians, architects, restorers, etc. 1827 edition. 59 plates. 114pp. 7⅞ x 10¾.
22236-5 Paperbound $3.50

DUTCH HOUSES IN THE HUDSON VALLEY BEFORE 1776, Helen Wilkinson Reynolds. The standard survey of the Dutch colonial house and outbuildings, with constructional features, decoration, and local history associated with individual homesteads. Introduction by Franklin D. Roosevelt. Map. 150 illustrations. 469pp. 6⅝ x 9¼.   21469-9 Paperbound $4.00

THE ARCHITECTURE OF COUNTRY HOUSES, Andrew J. Downing. Together with Vaux's *Villas and Cottages* this is the basic book for Hudson River Gothic architecture of the middle Victorian period. Full, sound discussions of general aspects of housing, architecture, style, decoration, furnishing, together with scores of detailed house plans, illustrations of specific buildings, accompanied by full text. Perhaps the most influential single American architectural book. 1850 edition. Introduction by J. Stewart Johnson. 321 figures, 34 architectural designs. xvi + 560pp.
22003-6 Paperbound $4.00

LOST EXAMPLES OF COLONIAL ARCHITECTURE, John Mead Howells. Full-page photographs of buildings that have disappeared or been so altered as to be denatured, including many designed by major early American architects. 245 plates. xvii + 248pp. 7⅞ x 10¾. 21143-6 Paperbound $3.00

DOMESTIC ARCHITECTURE OF THE AMERICAN COLONIES AND OF THE EARLY REPUBLIC, Fiske Kimball. Foremost architect and restorer of Williamsburg and Monticello covers nearly 200 homes between 1620-1825. Architectural details, construction, style features, special fixtures, floor plans, etc. Generally considered finest work in its area. 219 illustrations of houses, doorways, windows, capital mantels. xx + 314pp. 7⅞ x 10¾. 21743-4 Paperbound $3.50

EARLY AMERICAN ROOMS: 1650-1858, edited by Russell Hawes Kettell. Tour of 12 rooms, each representative of a different era in American history and each furnished, decorated, designed and occupied in the style of the era. 72 plans and elevations, 8-page color section, etc., show fabrics, wall papers, arrangements, etc. Full descriptive text. xvii + 200pp. of text. 8⅜ x 11¼. 21633-0 Paperbound $5.00

THE FITZWILLIAM VIRGINAL BOOK, edited by J. Fuller Maitland and W. B. Squire. Full modern printing of famous early 17th-century ms. volume of 300 works by Morley, Byrd, Bull, Gibbons, etc. For piano or other modern keyboard instrument; easy to read format. xxxvi + 938pp. 8⅜ x 11. 21068-5, 21069-3 Two volumes, Paperbound $8.00

HARPSICHORD MUSIC, Johann Sebastian Bach. Bach Gesellschaft edition. A rich selection of Bach's masterpieces for the harpsichord: the six English Suites, six French Suites, the six Partitas (Clavierübung part I), the Goldberg Variations (Clavierübung part IV), the fifteen Two-Part Inventions and the fifteen Three-Part Sinfonias. Clearly reproduced on large sheets with ample margins; eminently playable. vi + 312pp. 8⅛ x 11. 22360-4 Paperbound $5.00

THE MUSIC OF BACH: AN INTRODUCTION, Charles Sanford Terry. A fine, nontechnical introduction to Bach's music, both instrumental and vocal. Covers organ music, chamber music, passion music, other types. Analyzes themes, developments, innovations. x + 114pp. 21075-8 Paperbound $1.25

BEETHOVEN AND HIS NINE SYMPHONIES, Sir George Grove. Noted British musicologist provides best history, analysis, commentary on symphonies. Very thorough, rigorously accurate; necessary to both advanced student and amateur music lover. 436 musical passages. vii + 407 pp. 20334-4 Paperbound $2.25

JOHANN SEBASTIAN BACH, Philipp Spitta. One of the great classics of musicology, this definitive analysis of Bach's music (and life) has never been surpassed. Lucid, nontechnical analyses of hundreds of pieces (30 pages devoted to St. Matthew Passion, 26 to B Minor Mass). Also includes major analysis of 18th-century music. 450 musical examples. 40-page musical supplement. Total of xx + 1799pp.
(EUK) 22278-0, 22279-9 Two volumes, Clothbound $15.00

MOZART AND HIS PIANO CONCERTOS, Cuthbert Girdlestone. The only full-length study of an important area of Mozart's creativity. Provides detailed analyses of all 23 concertos, traces inspirational sources. 417 musical examples. Second edition. 509pp.
(USO) 21271-8 Paperbound $3.50

THE PERFECT WAGNERITE: A COMMENTARY ON THE NIBLUNG'S RING, George Bernard Shaw. Brilliant and still relevant criticism in remarkable essays on Wagner's Ring cycle, Shaw's ideas on political and social ideology behind the plots, role of Leitmotifs, vocal requisites, etc. Prefaces. xxi + 136pp.
21707-8 Paperbound $1.50

DON GIOVANNI, W. A. Mozart. Complete libretto, modern English translation; biographies of composer and librettist; accounts of early performances and critical reaction. Lavishly illustrated. All the material you need to understand and appreciate this great work. Dover Opera Guide and Libretto Series; translated and introduced by Ellen Bleiler. 92 illustrations. 209pp.
21134-7 Paperbound $1.50

HIGH FIDELITY SYSTEMS: A LAYMAN'S GUIDE, Roy F. Allison. All the basic information you need for setting up your own audio system: high fidelity and stereo record players, tape records, F.M. Connections, adjusting tone arm, cartridge, checking needle alignment, positioning speakers, phasing speakers, adjusting hums, trouble-shooting, maintenance, and similar topics. Enlarged 1965 edition. More than 50 charts, diagrams, photos. iv + 91pp.
21514-8 Paperbound $1.25

REPRODUCTION OF SOUND, Edgar Villchur. Thorough coverage for laymen of high fidelity systems, reproducing systems in general, needles, amplifiers, preamps, loudspeakers, feedback, explaining physical background. "A rare talent for making technicalities vividly comprehensible," R. Darrell, *High Fidelity.* 69 figures. iv + 92pp.
21515-6 Paperbound $1.00

HEAR ME TALKIN' TO YA: THE STORY OF JAZZ AS TOLD BY THE MEN WHO MADE IT, Nat Shapiro and Nat Hentoff. Louis Armstrong, Fats Waller, Jo Jones, Clarence Williams, Billy Holiday, Duke Ellington, Jelly Roll Morton and dozens of other jazz greats tell how it was in Chicago's South Side, New Orleans, depression Harlem and the modern West Coast as jazz was born and grew. xvi + 429pp.
21726-4 Paperbound $2.50

FABLES OF AESOP, translated by Sir Roger L'Estrange. A reproduction of the very rare 1931 Paris edition; a selection of the most interesting fables, together with 50 imaginative drawings by Alexander Calder. v + 128pp. 6½x9¼.
21780-9 Paperbound $1.25

EAST O' THE SUN AND WEST O' THE MOON, George W. Dasent. Considered the best of all translations of these Norwegian folk tales, this collection has been enjoyed by generations of children (and folklorists too). Includes True and Untrue, Why the Sea is Salt, East O' the Sun and West O' the Moon, Why the Bear is Stumpy-Tailed, Boots and the Troll, The Cock and the Hen, Rich Peter the Pedlar, and 52 more. The only edition with all 59 tales. 77 illustrations by Erik Werenskiold and Theodor Kittelsen. xv + 418pp. 22521-6 Paperbound $3.50

GOOPS AND HOW TO BE THEM, Gelett Burgess. Classic of tongue-in-cheek humor, masquerading as etiquette book. 87 verses, twice as many cartoons, show mischievous Goops as they demonstrate to children virtues of table manners, neatness, courtesy, etc. Favorite for generations. viii + 88pp. 6½ x 9¼. 22233-0 Paperbound $1.25

ALICE'S ADVENTURES UNDER GROUND, Lewis Carroll. The first version, quite different from the final *Alice in Wonderland,* printed out by Carroll himself with his own illustrations. Complete facsimile of the "million dollar" manuscript Carroll gave to Alice Liddell in 1864. Introduction by Martin Gardner. viii + 96pp. Title and dedication pages in color. 21482-6 Paperbound $1.25

THE BROWNIES, THEIR BOOK, Palmer Cox. Small as mice, cunning as foxes, exuberant and full of mischief, the Brownies go to the zoo, toy shop, seashore, circus, etc., in 24 verse adventures and 266 illustrations. Long a favorite, since their first appearance in St. Nicholas Magazine. xi + 144pp. 6⅝ x 9¼. 21265-3 Paperbound $1.75

SONGS OF CHILDHOOD, Walter De La Mare. Published (under the pseudonym Walter Ramal) when De La Mare was only 29, this charming collection has long been a favorite children's book. A facsimile of the first edition in paper, the 47 poems capture the simplicity of the nursery rhyme and the ballad, including such lyrics as I Met Eve, Tartary, The Silver Penny. vii + 106pp. 21972-0 Paperbound $1.25

THE COMPLETE NONSENSE OF EDWARD LEAR, Edward Lear. The finest 19th-century humorist-cartoonist in full: all nonsense limericks, zany alphabets, Owl and Pussycat, songs, nonsense botany, and more than 500 illustrations by Lear himself. Edited by Holbrook Jackson. xxix + 287pp. (USO) 20167-8 Paperbound $2.00

BILLY WHISKERS: THE AUTOBIOGRAPHY OF A GOAT, Frances Trego Montgomery. A favorite of children since the early 20th century, here are the escapades of that rambunctious, irresistible and mischievous goat—Billy Whiskers. Much in the spirit of *Peck's Bad Boy,* this is a book that children never tire of reading or hearing. All the original familiar illustrations by W. H. Fry are included: 6 color plates, 18 black and white drawings. 159pp. 22345-0 Paperbound $2.00

MOTHER GOOSE MELODIES. Faithful republication of the fabulously rare Munroe and Francis "copyright 1833" Boston edition—the most important Mother Goose collection, usually referred to as the "original." Familiar rhymes plus many rare ones, with wonderful old woodcut illustrations. Edited by E. F. Bleiler. 128pp. 4½ x 6⅜. 22577-1 Paperbound $1.25

TWO LITTLE SAVAGES; BEING THE ADVENTURES OF TWO BOYS WHO LIVED AS INDIANS AND WHAT THEY LEARNED, Ernest Thompson Seton. Great classic of nature and boyhood provides a vast range of woodlore in most palatable form, a genuinely entertaining story. Two farm boys build a teepee in woods and live in it for a month, working out Indian solutions to living problems, star lore, birds and animals, plants, etc. 293 illustrations. vii + 286pp.

20985-7 Paperbound $2.50

PETER PIPER'S PRACTICAL PRINCIPLES OF PLAIN & PERFECT PRONUNCIATION. Alliterative jingles and tongue-twisters of surprising charm, that made their first appearance in America about 1830. Republished in full with the spirited woodcut illustrations from this earliest American edition. 32pp. 4½ x 6⅜.

22560-7 Paperbound $1.00

SCIENCE EXPERIMENTS AND AMUSEMENTS FOR CHILDREN, Charles Vivian. 73 easy experiments, requiring only materials found at home or easily available, such as candles, coins, steel wool, etc.; illustrate basic phenomena like vacuum, simple chemical reaction, etc. All safe. Modern, well-planned. Formerly *Science Games for Children*. 102 photos, numerous drawings. 96pp. 6⅛ x 9¼.

21856-2 Paperbound $1.25

AN INTRODUCTION TO CHESS MOVES AND TACTICS SIMPLY EXPLAINED, Leonard Barden. Informal intermediate introduction, quite strong in explaining reasons for moves. Covers basic material, tactics, important openings, traps, positional play in middle game, end game. Attempts to isolate patterns and recurrent configurations. Formerly *Chess*. 58 figures. 102pp.   (USO) 21210-6 Paperbound $1.25

LASKER'S MANUAL OF CHESS, Dr. Emanuel Lasker. Lasker was not only one of the five great World Champions, he was also one of the ablest expositors, theorists, and analysts. In many ways, his Manual, permeated with his philosophy of battle, filled with keen insights, is one of the greatest works ever written on chess. Filled with analyzed games by the great players. A single-volume library that will profit almost any chess player, beginner or master. 308 diagrams. xli x 349pp.

20640-8 Paperbound $2.75

THE MASTER BOOK OF MATHEMATICAL RECREATIONS, Fred Schuh. In opinion of many the finest work ever prepared on mathematical puzzles, stunts, recreations; exhaustively thorough explanations of mathematics involved, analysis of effects, citation of puzzles and games. Mathematics involved is elementary. Translated by F. Göbel. 194 figures. xxiv + 430pp.   22134-2 Paperbound $3.00

MATHEMATICS, MAGIC AND MYSTERY, Martin Gardner. Puzzle editor for Scientific American explains mathematics behind various mystifying tricks: card tricks, stage "mind reading," coin and match tricks, counting out games, geometric dissections, etc. Probability sets, theory of numbers clearly explained. Also provides more than 400 tricks, guaranteed to work, that you can do. 135 illustrations. xii + 176pp.

20338-2 Paperbound $1.50

POEMS OF ANNE BRADSTREET, edited with an introduction by Robert Hutchinson. A new selection of poems by America's first poet and perhaps the first significant woman poet in the English language. 48 poems display her development in works of considerable variety—love poems, domestic poems, religious meditations, formal elegies, "quaternions," etc. Notes, bibliography. viii + 222pp.
22160-1 Paperbound $2.00

THREE GOTHIC NOVELS: THE CASTLE OF OTRANTO BY HORACE WALPOLE; VATHEK BY WILLIAM BECKFORD; THE VAMPYRE BY JOHN POLIDORI, WITH FRAGMENT OF A NOVEL BY LORD BYRON, edited by E. F. Bleiler. The first Gothic novel, by Walpole; the finest Oriental tale in English, by Beckford; powerful Romantic supernatural story in versions by Polidori and Byron. All extremely important in history of literature; all still exciting, packed with supernatural thrills, ghosts, haunted castles, magic, etc. xl + 291pp.
21232-7 Paperbound $2.50

THE BEST TALES OF HOFFMANN, E. T. A. Hoffmann. 10 of Hoffmann's most important stories, in modern re-editings of standard translations: Nutcracker and the King of Mice, Signor Formica, Automata, The Sandman, Rath Krespel, The Golden Flowerpot, Master Martin the Cooper, The Mines of Falun, The King's Betrothed, A New Year's Eve Adventure. 7 illustrations by Hoffmann. Edited by E. F. Bleiler. xxxix + 419pp.   21793-0 Paperbound $3.00

GHOST AND HORROR STORIES OF AMBROSE BIERCE, Ambrose Bierce. 23 strikingly modern stories of the horrors latent in the human mind: The Eyes of the Panther, The Damned Thing, An Occurrence at Owl Creek Bridge, An Inhabitant of Carcosa, etc., plus the dream-essay, Visions of the Night. Edited by E. F. Bleiler. xxii + 199pp.   20767-6 Paperbound $1.50

BEST GHOST STORIES OF J. S. LEFANU, J. Sheridan LeFanu. Finest stories by Victorian master often considered greatest supernatural writer of all. Carmilla, Green Tea, The Haunted Baronet, The Familiar, and 12 others. Most never before available in the U. S. A. Edited by E. F. Bleiler. 8 illustrations from Victorian publications. xvii + 467pp.   20415-4 Paperbound $3.00

MATHEMATICAL FOUNDATIONS OF INFORMATION THEORY, A. I. Khinchin. Comprehensive introduction to work of Shannon, McMillan, Feinstein and Khinchin, placing these investigations on a rigorous mathematical basis. Covers entropy concept in probability theory, uniqueness theorem, Shannon's inequality, ergodic sources, the E property, martingale concept, noise, Feinstein's fundamental lemma, Shanon's first and second theorems. Translated by R. A. Silverman and M. D. Friedman. iii + 120pp.   60434-9 Paperbound $1.75

SEVEN SCIENCE FICTION NOVELS, H. G. Wells. The standard collection of the great novels. Complete, unabridged. *First Men in the Moon, Island of Dr. Moreau, War of the Worlds, Food of the Gods, Invisible Man, Time Machine, In the Days of the Comet.* Not only science fiction fans, but every educated person owes it to himself to read these novels. 1015pp.   20264-X Clothbound $5.00

ADVENTURES OF AN AFRICAN SLAVER, Theodore Canot. Edited by Brantz Mayer. A detailed portrayal of slavery and the slave trade, 1820-1840. Canot, an established trader along the African coast, describes the slave economy of the African kingdoms, the treatment of captured negroes, the extensive journeys in the interior to gather slaves, slave revolts and their suppression, harems, bribes, and much more. Full and unabridged republication of 1854 edition. Introduction by Malcom Cowley. 16 illustrations. xvii + 448pp. 22456-2 Paperbound $3.50

MY BONDAGE AND MY FREEDOM, Frederick Douglass. Born and brought up in slavery, Douglass witnessed its horrors and experienced its cruelties, but went on to become one of the most outspoken forces in the American anti-slavery movement. Considered the best of his autobiographies, this book graphically describes the inhuman treatment of slaves, its effects on slave owners and slave families, and how Douglass's determination led him to a new life. Unaltered reprint of 1st (1855) edition. xxxii + 464pp. 22457-0 Paperbound $2.50

THE INDIANS' BOOK, recorded and edited by Natalie Curtis. Lore, music, narratives, dozens of drawings by Indians themselves from an authoritative and important survey of native culture among Plains, Southwestern, Lake and Pueblo Indians. Standard work in popular ethnomusicology. 149 songs in full notation. 23 drawings, 23 photos. xxxi + 584pp. 6⅝ x 9⅜. 21939-9 Paperbound $4.50

DICTIONARY OF AMERICAN PORTRAITS, edited by Hayward and Blanche Cirker. 4024 portraits of 4000 most important Americans, colonial days to 1905 (with a few important categories, like Presidents, to present). Pioneers, explorers, colonial figures, U. S. officials, politicians, writers, military and naval men, scientists, inventors, manufacturers, jurists, actors, historians, educators, notorious figures, Indian chiefs, etc. All authentic contemporary likenesses. The only work of its kind in existence; supplements all biographical sources for libraries. Indispensable to anyone working with American history. 8,000-item classified index, finding lists, other aids. xiv + 756pp. 9¼ x 12¾. 21823-6 Clothbound $30.00

TRITTON'S GUIDE TO BETTER WINE AND BEER MAKING FOR BEGINNERS, S. M. Tritton. All you need to know to make family-sized quantities of over 100 types of grape, fruit, herb and vegetable wines; as well as beers, mead, cider, etc. Complete recipes, advice as to equipment, procedures such as fermenting, bottling, and storing wines. Recipes given in British, U. S., and metric measures. Accompanying booklet lists sources in U. S. A. where ingredients may be bought, and additional information. 11 illustrations. 157pp. 5⅝ x 8⅛. (USO) 22090-7 Clothbound $3.50

GARDENING WITH HERBS FOR FLAVOR AND FRAGRANCE, Helen M. Fox. How to grow herbs in your own garden, how to use them in your cooking (over 55 recipes included), legends and myths associated with each species, uses in medicine, perfumes, etc.—these are elements of one of the few books written especially for American herb fanciers. Guides you step-by-step from soil preparation to harvesting and storage for each type of herb. 12 drawings by Louise Mansfield. xiv + 334pp. 22540-2 Paperbound $2.50

MATHEMATICAL PUZZLES FOR BEGINNERS AND ENTHUSIASTS, Geoffrey Mott-Smith. 189 puzzles from easy to difficult—involving arithmetic, logic, algebra, properties of digits, probability, etc.—for enjoyment and mental stimulus. Explanation of mathematical principles behind the puzzles. 135 illustrations. viii + 248pp.
20198-8 Paperbound $1.75

PAPER FOLDING FOR BEGINNERS, William D. Murray and Francis J. Rigney. Easiest book on the market, clearest instructions on making interesting, beautiful origami. Sail boats, cups, roosters, frogs that move legs, bonbon boxes, standing birds, etc. 40 projects; more than 275 diagrams and photographs. 94pp.
20713-7 Paperbound $1.00

TRICKS AND GAMES ON THE POOL TABLE, Fred Herrmann. 79 tricks and games— some solitaires, some for two or more players, some competitive games—to entertain you between formal games. Mystifying shots and throws, unusual caroms, tricks involving such props as cork, coins, a hat, etc. Formerly *Fun on the Pool Table.* 77 figures. 95pp.
21814-7 Paperbound $1.00

HAND SHADOWS TO BE THROWN UPON THE WALL: A SERIES OF NOVEL AND AMUSING FIGURES FORMED BY THE HAND, Henry Bursill. Delightful picturebook from great-grandfather's day shows how to make 18 different hand shadows: a bird that flies, duck that quacks, dog that wags his tail, camel, goose, deer, boy, turtle, etc. Only book of its sort. vi + 33pp. 6½ x 9¼.   21779-5 Paperbound $1.00

WHITTLING AND WOODCARVING, E. J. Tangerman. 18th printing of best book on market. "If you can cut a potato you can carve" toys and puzzles, chains, chessmen, caricatures, masks, frames, woodcut blocks, surface patterns, much more. Information on tools, woods, techniques. Also goes into serious wood sculpture from Middle Ages to present, East and West. 464 photos, figures. x + 293pp.
20965-2 Paperbound $2.00

HISTORY OF PHILOSOPHY, Julián Marías. Possibly the clearest, most easily followed, best planned, most useful one-volume history of philosophy on the market; neither skimpy nor overfull. Full details on system of every major philosopher and dozens of less important thinkers from pre-Socratics up to Existentialism and later. Strong on many European figures usually omitted. Has gone through dozens of editions in Europe. 1966 edition, translated by Stanley Appelbaum and Clarence Strowbridge. xviii + 505pp.   21739-6 Paperbound $3.00

YOGA: A SCIENTIFIC EVALUATION, Kovoor T. Behanan. Scientific but non-technical study of physiological results of yoga exercises; done under auspices of Yale U. Relations to Indian thought, to psychoanalysis, etc. 16 photos. xxiii + 270pp.
20505-3 Paperbound $2.50

Prices subject to change without notice.
Available at your book dealer or write for free catalogue to Dept. GI, Dover Publications, Inc., 180 Varick St., N. Y., N. Y. 10014. Dover publishes more than 150 books each year on science, elementary and advanced mathematics, biology, music, art, literary history, social sciences and other areas.